Model United Nations:
An Essential Guide for Students
Preparing for Simulation Conferences

Jeffrey S. Morton

Model United Nations:
An Essential Guide for Students
Preparing for Simulation Conferences

Jeffrey S. Morton

Academica Press
Washington

Library of Congress Cataloging-in-Publication Data

Names: Morton, Jeffrey (author)

Title: Model united nations : an essential guide for students preparing for simulation conferences | Morton, Jeffrey.

Description: Washington : Academica Press, 2025.

Identifiers: LCCN 2025945981 | ISBN 9781680533576 (hardcover) | ISBN 9781680533583 (ebook)

Contents

About the Author

Jeffrey S. Morton is the Pierrepont-Comfort Chair of Political Science at Florida Atlantic University and a Fellow at the Foreign Policy Association. He received his Master of Arts from Rutgers University, specializing in war studies, and his Ph.D. from the University of South Carolina in international law. His United Nations experience includes the summer training program offered by the International Law Commission (ILC) in Geneva, a graduate research internship at the United Nations Educational, Scientific & Cultural Organization (UNESCO) in Paris, and a posting in the Office of the Under-Secretary General for Political Affairs at UN headquarters in New York.

Dr. Morton established the Leon Charney Diplomacy Program at FAU in 1996. His university has received more than eighty national and international delegation awards in model diplomacy conferences.

Acknowledgements

I would like to begin by thanking the faculty and administrative staff at Florida Atlantic University for providing unparalleled levels of support through the decades. When I proposed teaching a Model United Nations class in 1996, there was nothing but encouragement from my colleagues. Over time, the university allowed me the latitude to build and develop the Diplomacy Program in ways that I saw fit. Dean Manju Pendakur, in 2008, authorized me to fundraise for the Program, an opportunity rarely afforded to faculty. I thank Tzili Charney for her inspiration and support, most notably the naming gift that she provided. I thank Drs. Timothy Steigenga and Luisa Turbino Torres for serving as Associate Directors of the program.

I would be remiss to not thank Dr. Cheryl Brown at the University of North Carolina-Charlotte, my first Model United Nations teacher. The preparation format that is found in this manual was greatly influenced by her training approach and mirrors the seriousness and professionalism that she exhibited. I genuinely thank the executive leadership at the National Model United Nations organization for the amazing conferences that they organize multiple times each year. Without them, there would be no national conference to inspire college students from all over the world to actively engage in the resolution of the many challenges that the international community faces. Michael Eaton, Executive Director of the National Model United Nations, was kind enough to review the manuscript and offer useful suggestions that were incorporated in the final draft.

No acknowledgment would be complete without a reference to the thousands of students who have participated in my program at FAU. While most have pursued careers distinct from diplomacy, others have seen their professional trajectories redirected towards international affairs. They have gone on to careers in the U.S. State Department, Department of Defense, Central Intelligence Agency, Secret Service, United Nations and more than a few went on to become college professors who are currently directing Model UN programs of their own.

Finally, thank you to Katherine McMillan, my graduate teaching assistant who has reviewed this manuscript and offered incredibly insightful suggestions that have made their way into the final draft.

Foreword

Model diplomacy simulations offer students opportunities to develop practical skills (research, debate, document drafting and public speaking) and implement them while negotiating with others, typically in one common language. There is an inherent bias away from isolationism since the point is to engage with others while discussing pending global issues from the perspective of an assigned country. Those who go on to work in diplomacy, including at the United Nations, routinely comment on how accurate the Model UN process is. And whether a simulation is in the classroom or at an organized conference, the experiential learning of trying one's hand at diplomacy offers students insights into the difficulty of finding compromise and multilateral solutions.

Professor Morton's text shares forty years of experience in a succinct format that answers the most common question from both student leaders of club programs and faculty advisors at those for academic credit – how to prepare?! For any team, practice is a means of improvement. And Professor Morton offers a clear guide to the exercises that he has continued to revise while leaving space for others to adapt to their own academic environment (for example, his program allows students to attend a conference once so he does not have the option to pair veteran and new students as others might, though he argues for a more egalitarian approach regardless). Most remarkable, each of the twelve weeks of preparation includes their own simulation on a topic that does not require prepared research to help students build confidence in their developing skills.

The twelve-week timeline for preparation is valuable regardless of whether participation is graded. For those preparing in a classroom, there are sample quizzes and exams as well as suggested point totals. As a conference organizer of what is labeled an academic conference, let me express my appreciation for the emphasis on grading on preparation and participation, not at-conference activities such as the number of speeches given or working paper co-sponsorships which can impact the discussions if a peer is asking to be involved for a grade rather than interest in the topic. And while awards are a useful fundraising tool, I appreciate the lack of emphasis he gives them since no methodology can accurately reflect the learning and growth of attendees.

Most unique, Professor Morton also shares a variety of fundraising models he has used successfully at Florida Atlantic University to minimize costs to students. They include individual scholarships from community members and working with the administration on endowed gifts. It is worth noting that despite the hyper-partisan political environment, there has been strong support for the skill development achieved in model diplomacy even if not for the agenda of all aspects of the contemporary agenda of the international organizations simulated.

Both veterans of Model United Nations programs as well as new leaders will benefit greatly from this distillation of 40+ years of experience training outstanding student delegates into twelve weeks of hands-on preparation activities that can be used for high school or university level conference preparation. On behalf of the Model Diplomacy community – thank you Professor Morton for sharing this extension of your academic teaching and learning legacy.

– Michael Eaton, Executive Director, National Model UN

Introduction

Model diplomacy is a popular and highly effective teaching tool used in middle school, high school, college and university classes. Diplomatic simulations may be incorporated into a class as a portion of the overall set of assignments or may be used to prepare students to participate in formal simulation conferences. Model diplomacy teaches public speaking, research, debate, teamwork and conflict resolution. Teaching model diplomacy allows for the employment of a "flipped classroom" strategy of instruction. In the traditional instruction style, students are taught substantive material in class and then assigned homework that reinforces what they have learned. In the flipped strategy, the students acquire the substantive information (world politics, country background, specialized topics) outside the classroom and apply that knowledge in exercises and simulations administered in class. This approach encourages students to be stakeholders in the learning process as opposed to simply receiving information through instruction and demonstration of mastery on exams.

While model diplomacy, in the classroom or at a competitive conference, varies greatly in terms of intensity, duration and grounding in real world politics, it is built upon a set of common attributes. Students are assigned a country to represent in a simulated world politics challenge. They deliver speeches during formal sessions and negotiate with others during informal, or caucus, sessions. At the conclusion of the simulation, resolutions drafted by groups of student-delegates are presented to the whole for final consideration and a vote. Throughout the process, rules of procedure are used to maintain order and allow all representatives the opportunity to fully participate. Students are expected to remain in country character, accurately representing their government's positions, and in diplomatic character, acting in ways that reflect established protocol, throughout the conference.

The simulation topic may parallel a current world politics issue, a historical event or a manufactured situation. Except in crisis simulations, students are given notice of the simulated challenge and encouraged to prepare in advance. In crisis simulations, topic details are provided when the simulation begins. In either case, students are expected to have sufficient knowledge of their assigned country's foreign policy and interests to accurately represent it during the proceedings. Properly prepared student-delegates will have studied their country's history, government, society, economy and foreign relations. In addition to understanding the country that they are assigned, students should be trained in diplomatic protocol, rules of procedure and proper strategies employed to negotiate with other delegates. Finally, a fully prepared student-delegate will be able to think critically, analytically and creatively about the issue that is being considered in the simulation.

The purpose of this prep manual is to provide instructors, group leaders and students, from middle school to university, with a blueprint to prepare for model diplomacy simulations, with a particular focus on Model United Nations (MUN). Information and strategies found herein will be useful for instructors who want to use model diplomacy to supplement a wide range of courses as well as those who direct and manage programs that send delegations to formal conferences.

This project is the product of more than forty years of model diplomacy experience. I attended my first MUN conference in Los Angeles in 1983, representing Israel as part of a model UN club with no instructor and minimal preparation. Our group of seven undergraduates met once to receive our country and committee assignments and were wished the best of luck by the advisor along with a stern warning to be on our best behavior at the conference. The one-day conference was a whirlwind, dominated by students who had model diplomatic experience. I attended that first conference without any prepared notes or speeches and mainly watched the sessions unfold to conclusion.

The Model United Nations of the Far West in Sacramento, California was held a few months later. The same small delegation attended with a much greater understanding of what was expected and how to navigate the conference. After transferring to an East Coast school, I was delighted to see a flier advertising try-outs for the Model UN club. After being selected,

I participated in the New York NMUN conference as a member of a formal program that required a three-credit upper-division course with high expectations. During my doctoral studies, I served as the graduate advisor of the university's Model UN club and chaperoned students to the New York conference. As a professor, I founded the Diplomacy Program at Florida Atlantic University in 1996. I have prepared undergraduates to participate in regional, national and international model diplomacy conferences. My students have attended conferences across the United States, Europe and Asia. They have competed in Model United Nations, Model European Union, Model Organization of American States and Model NATO conferences.

In 2016, the program was named in honor of Leon Charney. Mr. Charney was a successful real estate developer who played a key role as a backdoor channel for President Carter during the Camp David negotiations in the 1970s that resulted in an Accord that stabilized relations between Israel and Egypt. The accompanied endowed gift allowed the program to operate year-round in three colleges at the university. It participates in the National Model United Nations simulations in Washington, D.C. in the fall and in New York City in the spring. The 2025 D.C. delegation was comprised of 100 undergraduate students, ranging from first-year students to seniors, representing eleven majors. The skills taught in diplomacy classes are valuable assets for students pursuing careers in diplomacy, law, education, business, nursing, engineering, among many others. I have always believed that the true measure of a model diplomacy program's success is the degree to which students grow as individuals throughout the training protocol and conference participation. Awards received at the conference, while critically important for fundraising purposes and student résumés, are secondary in importance.

This prep manual outlines twelve lesson plans that are each divided into two sections. Sessions labeled "A" are designed to teach students the most important skills necessary for successful model diplomacy participation. Homework assignments and in-class activities hone public speaking skills, negotiating tactics and teach diplomatic protocol and decorum. Sessions labeled "B" are simulations that sharpen the skills learned in the A sessions. Simulating crises and problem solving is essential to successfully preparing students for a model diplomacy conference. Ultimately, all the research that goes into a delegation's preparation and the skills taught in class are put to the test at the conference. Simulations for the sake of simulations are of minimal value, each one must contain teaching opportunities that improve the skill sets of the students. Post-simulation debriefing is key to the learning process. Each simulation is designed to teach one or more techniques and lessons to the students, as explained after each simulation's presentation.

The simulations are presented in a specific order, designed to train students with a solid foundation and then building from there. At the conclusion of the training protocol, students will be optimally prepared for a conference. This manual takes instructors and students through the full process of developing, organizing, managing and entry into conference of a model diplomacy program. Once complete, students will be ready to participate in the most prestigious and demanding conferences.

International Organization

The interactions between countries, or nation-states, create opportunities, challenges and problems that must be addressed. Examples of interactions include trade, international travel, armed conflict, climate change and territorial disputes, among many others. The state may opt to deal with the issue without the input or participation from others, referred to as unilateralism, or work with other states. When multilateralism is used to resolve an issue, international organization (IO) occurs. The golden age of IO is the period between the Congress of Vienna (1815) and the establishment of the League of Nations (1919). The international organization process involves several stages. First, nations meet to discuss an issue of concern and debate how to revolve or mitigate it. If successful, they draft an agreement, or treaty, that lays out their duties and responsibilities to address the issue. Next, they build an organizational structure that allows them to periodically meet to monitor progress and make necessary revisions to the original agreement. Finally, the organization operates in its effort to continually address the issue of concern. During the Golden Age of IO, hundreds of organizations were created, some of which remain in operation today. Organizations made up of individuals are referred to as Non-Governmental Organizations (NGOs), while those whose members are nation-states are Intergovernmental Organizations (IOs). The United Nations and NATO are examples of intergovernmental organizations.

It was the failure of the League of Nations (LON) to prevent the onset of the Second World War that effectively ended the Golden Age. Long before WWII ended, however, leading states began the process of designing the League's successor and established the United Nations (UN) in 1945. The leaders of the United States, Soviet Union and the United Kingdom met several times to reach a consensus on where the new IO would be located, how it would be structured and its powers. Diplomats then hammered out the UN Charter, which was signed in 1945 and ratified by fifty-one states, the original members.

The United Nations

The United Nations was built upon an expanded version of the structure of the League. The LON's Assembly, where all member-states met to discuss issues of concern, was renamed the General Assembly. The Council, limited in membership and responsible for addressing serious security problems became the Security Council. The League's Permanent Court of International Justice (PCIJ) was kept and renamed the International Court of Justice (ICJ). Both the League and United Nations included an administrative building, which is referred to as the Secretariat. Additionally, the United Nations added two new principal organs. The Economic and Social Council (ECOSOC) was designed to promote the development of countries in Africa, Asia and Latin America and the Trusteeship Council (TC) was charged with assisting colonial possessions in their efforts to become independent. The UN also created a series of commissions, specialized agencies and programmes, each with its assigned duties.

The United Nations, like all international organizations, is an instrument available to states to resolve problems and advance interests. It is as powerful, or weak, as states allow it. The common mistake is for observers to expect the United Nations to do something about a threat to peace or an international injustice. The organization succeeds when its member-states align their interests with each other and use the body to reach a resolution. Students who participate in Model United Nations conferences must prioritize their state's interests while attempting to find common ground with other delegates to reach agreement. It is a delicate balance that must be maintained and the challenge that makes model diplomacy conferences so interesting.

Other Notable Organizations

While most model diplomacy conferences simulate the United Nations and its vast agenda, other international organizations are simulated as well. Model NATO conferences simulate the North Atlantic Treaty Organization, which was created by the United States and its allies after World War II to counter Soviet aggression in Europe. With the end of the Cold War, NATO's membership expanded, and its agenda broadened. Model NATO conferences include thirty-two members and consider issues ranging from armed intervention to counter-terrorism to capacity building outside of Western Europe and North America. The European Union (EU), an integration process that began shortly after World War II, is also a popular organization for model diplomacy conferences. Except for the exit of the United Kingdom (BREXIT), membership in the EU has grown steadily. With a goal of promoting peace, freedom and justice, the agenda of the European Union is broad and encompassing. Other regional organizations, such as the African Union, the Arab League and the Organization of American States, are frequently simulated by student-delegates in model diplomacy conferences.

Before the First Meeting of the Group

The teacher or group leader has quite a bit of work to do prior to the first meeting with students. The most important tasks are to become acquainted with model diplomacy as an educational activity, register for a model diplomacy conference and prepare the research binders. Each is addressed below.

Understanding Model Diplomacy

The concept model diplomacy (MD) encompasses any organized session where individuals role-play political, social or economic actors in a simulation of a real world or manufactured situation. It is broader than the commonly used term Model United Nations, which is limited to simulating a specific international organization. Model diplomacy captures not only simulations of the United Nations (UN) but also other inter-governmental organizations (NATO, OAS, Arab League, European Union, African Union, IMF), historical periods (Congress of Vienna, July Crisis of 1914, the Berlin Crisis of 1948) and wholly fabricated arenas and interactions (Game of Thrones, Lord of the Rings, Star Wars, and the like). Model diplomacy conferences can be divided into three distinct categories, as explained below. Selecting the right type of conference for your school and students is critically important since preparation for each varies greatly.

Academic Conferences

While all model diplomacy conferences are 'academic' to an extent since they are attended by students, an academic conference is one which has attributes that distinguish itself from the Social and Fantasy conferences. A conference qualifies as academic if its aim is to accurately reflect the processes undertaken by the institutions that it is simulating and takes steps to ensure that student-delegates are held to those expectations. The topics considered are serious and material to the organization, preparation guides provided are accurate and detailed, members of the dais correctly use the rules of order and final documents are held to high standards of quality. Judging at academic conferences is performed by knowledgeable and experienced staff and points are awarded based upon objective diplomatic process standards.

Most academic conferences are overseen by organizations with extensive experience setting up and managing conferences and are attended by students who attend for-credit classes or faculty-led clubs that prepare them for the simulation. Preparation for participation in an academic conference entails extensive reviews of country policies and topic backgrounds. Position papers and speeches are normally prepared in advance of the simulation, but most academic conferences do not allow pre-drafted resolutions. The basic idea of the conference is to allow well-prepared students to openly, accurately and professionally debate the topics and attempt to resolve them in conjunction with other student-delegates. Diplomatic decorum is expected at the conference and guidance is provided by the dais to assist student-delegates in maneuvering through the cumbersome diplomatic process.

The oldest, largest and most prestigious academic model diplomacy is National Model United Nations (NMUN), which hosts conferences in Washington, D.C. in the fall, New York City in the spring and offers an annual international conference. It is a recognized Non-Governmental Organization (NGO) formally associated with the United Nations Department of Global Communications and an NGO in consultative status with the United Nations Department of Economic and Social Affairs. NMUN, or Nationals, is open to colleges and universities around the world. Data presented by NMUN indicates that in 2022 its conferences were attended by more than 4,000 students from 240 colleges and universities internationally. The NMUN conference in New York is by far the largest academic conference, both in terms of the number of participants and the number of committees simulated. NMUN's Washington conference is smaller, simulating eight committees for approximately 1,000 students while maintaining the organization's high standards.

Academic conferences can be found in most every U.S. state and abroad. An excellent source of information about the academic conferences is the United Nations Association of the United States of America (UNA-USA). Its webpage offers useful resources and its calendar of conferences demonstrates the popularity of model diplomacy. For those interested in traveling abroad for a conference, numerous quality offerings can be found in Europe, Asia, Latin America and Africa.

Social Conferences

A social model diplomacy is one that downplays the importance of preparation, accurate country representation and quality of drafted documents. Most social conferences are hosted by universities and organized by students, as opposed to the professional staff employed by the organizations who host academic conferences. What is emphasized is the ability to use the rules of procedure effectively and building a following of other delegates in committee. Social conferences are primarily about swaying opinion as opposed to paralleling real-world country interactions.

Choosing a social conference fundamentally changes the way that a diplomacy program is organized and managed. The type of student that is recruited for successful programs is different. For academic programs, we tend to value scholastic accomplishment, consistency, a solid work ethic, the ability to follow rules and listen to instruction. For social conference participation, the best students are those who are outgoing, persuasive and have an outsized level of self-confidence. Despite the differences in approach, however, social conference participants will benefit from the exercises and simulations found in this training manual.

Social conferences have a circuit of conferences where points, golden gavels and awards count towards rankings that are meticulously updated and posted. The key to a high placement in the rankings is volume of conferences. Because academic programs emphasize formal training and thorough preparation, it is common to participate in one conference per semester. Such limitations do not apply to social diplomacy programs. It is not unusual for those schools to travel to twelve or more conferences per academic year, often times sending the same students to attend two conferences on successive weekends. A student from a social program once told me that he represented Saudi Arabia on the World Tourism Commission (WTC) and four days later represented Brazil on ECOSOC. I didn't need to ask him how much preparation went into country, committee and topic backgrounds as the answer was obvious.

The major advantage that social programs enjoy over academic is access to student government funding. Because they do not have an academic class or instructor, they qualify as social and cultural activities that can be funded through student government funds. Many schools have no choice but to attend model diplomacy conferences as a social program.

Fantasy Conferences

The divide between serious academic model diplomacy programs and the more argumentative, social-oriented programs is as old as model diplomacy. In recent decades, a new approach to model conferences has emerged that is rapidly growing in popularity. Rather than being restricted by diplomatic norms and protocols, students have found a more expressive experience by attending fantasy conferences. In these settings, real world challenges are dismissed as is the real world itself. Organizers select a theme, usually reflecting a popular movie series or book. Student "delegates" take on the persona of one of the characters. Harry Potter, Star Wars, Lord of the Rings, Avatar and Pirates of the Caribbean have been among the most popular of the fantasy conferences. Not surprisingly, dressing as the assigned character is an important part of participating. It is best described as Comicon meets the United Nations. As trivial as the fantasy conferences sound, their growing popularity at the expense of the academic and quasi-academic/social conferences cannot be dismissed.

Registering for a Conference

Having selected the type of conference (academic, social, fantasy) to attend, it is time to register your group. Model diplomacy conferences take place throughout the academic year across the nation and abroad. Local conferences are often organized by model diplomacy programs as a means of fundraising and typically involve schools and clubs from the immediate area. Regional conferences, such as the Southern Regional Model United Nations (SRMUN) in Atlanta, Model United Nations of the Far West (MUNFW) in San Francisco and Model European Union (MEU) in Indianapolis, are but a few of the dozens of model diplomacies in this category. Finally, there are the national conferences that attract participants from across the country and around the world. The National Model United Nations is the most prominent of conferences in this category, attracting students from hundreds of colleges and universities from every continent. While the reputation, size and status of the conference are important variables to consider when selecting where to take your students, the most important determinant is your budget. Traveling to Chicago to attend the American Model United Nations International (AMUNI) may offer your group the most exciting academic trip, however, the cost of attendance may not fit in your budget. Whether yours is a new or established model diplomacy group, don't break the bank to attend one particular conference or travel to an exciting host city. Make a careful review of your financial situation and opt for a conference whose total expenses are 90% or less of your expected available funds. After the training protocol, you will find a chapter on financing a model diplomacy program and fundraising principles to follow. It is better to start out modestly and surpass your financial goals than to aim too high and fall short.

Once you have selected the appropriate conference for your students and your budget, follow the online prompts to register the group while being mindful of the stated deadlines (registration, fees, hotel rooms, position papers, etc.). An important decision that must be made at the time of registration is country selection. There is a general misperception about the importance of country assignment for model diplomacy conferences. It is commonly believed that the assignment is a reflection of program status and expected contribution to the conference proceedings. Accordingly, many more requests are made for high-profile assignments (United States, Russia, China, United Kingdom) than low-profile countries (Honduras, Cambodia, Cote D'Ivoire). This misperception about country assignment should not only be dismissed but turned on its head.

In reality, the higher the name recognition of the assigned country, the higher the expectation of performance. Everyone can identify France as a major actor in world affairs and expect the French delegation to take a leading role in the adjudication of many international problems. Representing a less known country, such as Azerbaijan, does not carry with it the same unreasonable expectations from fellow delegates. It is logical to conclude that it is easier to exceed low expectations than to meet and surpass high expectations.

Rather than selecting a country based upon name recognition or personal preference, opt for one that can uniquely stand out in committee. Island nations (Sri Lanka, Bahamas, Cabo Verde, etc.) are often overlooked in the selection process, yet they offer boundless opportunities for their representatives to stand out. Take Cyprus as an example. A Mediterranean country that is sandwiched geographically between Europe, Africa and Asia, Cyprus has a logical tie to multiple regions and, as an island nation, can connect with others to form an Island Nation working group. Honduras is another example of a country that crosses many bloc lines. It is a Central American state, a member of Latin America and is a Caribbean nation. The most important factor in selecting a country to represent at the conference, however, is delegation size. Small conferences may simulate as few as three committees, while large ones can organize more than a dozen. The 2025 NMUN-NYC conference simulated sixteen committees. Since not all countries are represented on all committees, assignments ranged at the conference from six to sixteen. At most conferences, students are allowed to double-up on committee. In that case, a country represented on ten committees can have as many as twenty students assigned to it. After verifying that placing two students on committees is allowed, divide the number of students in your group by two to determine which countries to consider representing. I advise against selecting a country that is assigned to the same number of committees as you have students, meaning that your school will place one student-delegate on each committee. It is better to place two students on each committee to guarantee representation if one of your students declines to travel to the conference or falls ill during the proceedings. Research binders, discussed below, will be distributed during the first meeting of the group. It is then that students will learn of their assigned country. If your group requires multiple country assignments, divide the students accordingly in advance of the first meeting.

Research Binder Prep

The binders, or research portfolios, should be prepped in advance by the instructor or students in the club. The research binder is an important component of the learning process. In my program, we use a 2" binder with the assigned country's name on the spine and a cover that identifies its owner as a member of The Permanent Mission of COUNTRY NAME to the United Nations. Smaller binders (1", ½") are perfectly fine and are more common. An example of the binder cover is provided at the end of this chapter.

Place a printed placard with the name of the student in the inside sleeve. The first purpose of the binder is to serve as a measure of student preparation across the twelve-week preparation period. The second purpose is to enhance student confidence that they are making progress towards being ready for the conference. As they see the binder increasingly filled with information about their assigned country, committee topics and formal speeches, they will be reassured that they are moving in the right direction. The third purpose of the research portfolio is to enhance conference performance. Students will rely upon the binder as they are negotiating with fellow delegates and begin drafting working papers and resolutions. An added, and important, advantage of having an impressive and well-organized binder is the effect that it has on delegates from other schools. The portfolio signals to fellow delegates that your student is serious and prepared to engage the topics and seek a resolution of the assigned challenges. Periodic binder checks give the students benchmark goals for completing their research, the check dates and the information needed at each stage are provided at the appropriate time in this manual.

What follows is a twelve-week training protocol that is designed to take a group of students from the starting gate to a polished delegation ready for an academic conference. The teaching plan is designed for two hours of classroom time per week. You have the option of breaking the meetings up into two 60-minute sessions or weekly two-hour sessions. Each week's plan of action is divided into two sections: skills building and simulations.

PERMANENT MISSION OF THE FEDERAL REPUBLIC OF GERMANY TO THE UNITED NATIONS

GENERAL ASSEMBLY THIRD

The Twelve-Week Preparation Schedule

	Skills Training	Simulations
Week 1	Self-Introductions Name Tags & Binders Review NMUN Trip Goals & Priorities	Matter of Urgent Importance
Week 2	Country Speeches Map Quiz Purposes of a Speech Travel Documents Committee Assignments	Fatal Decision
Week 3	Map Quiz Position Paper Intro What Would You Do?	City Selection
Week 4	Portfolio Check #1 Map Quiz Country Knowledge Quiz Resolution Clauses	Water Rights
Week 5	Map Quiz Agenda Speech Staying in Character	Self-Determination
Week 6	1st Topic Speech Wedge Issues Review Rules of Order	Trust or Betrayal
Week 7	Position Paper Drafts Portfolio Check #2	Crisis in Africa
Week 8	"Hot Seat" Wedge Issues 2nd Topic Speech	Revolution
Week 9	Portfolio Check #3 "Hot Seat II"	OPEC+ Summit
Week 10	Korean Peninsula I	Korean Peninsula II
Week 11	Mid-Term Exam	Divided Island I
Week 12	Divided Island II	Tsunami

In order to keep track of student progress and for final grading purposes, I use the grade sheet shown below. One sheet is printed for each student.

Grade Sheet

Name _____

Attendance: 200 points

              1A 1B 2A 2B 3A 3B 4A 4B 5A 5B

              6A 6B 7A 7B 8A 8B 9A 9B 10A 10B

*Attendance is taken beginning in Week 2 and continues through Week 11

Nine points for each class attended on time, one point for having placard. One point will be deducted for late arrival of three minutes or less, two points deducted for arriving more than three minutes late.

Geography Quizzes: 10 points each   1 2 3 4

Prepared Speeches: 10 points each   1 2 3

Position Papers: 100 points

Portfolio Checks: First (30 points)   Second (40)   Third (60)

Simulations: 20 points each   1   2   3   4   5   6

                             7   8   9   10   11   12

Mid-Term Examination: 60 points

Conference: 100 points*

Final Exam: 100

Total # of Points: /1000

*Conference points are awarded for attendance of required sessions and remaining in diplomatic character during the conference. It is a violation of most conference rules to grade students based upon the number of resolutions drafted and/or passed or the number of times that they delivered formal speeches.

Week 1A

Getting the Ball Rolling

Getting off to the right start is significantly more important than getting off to a fast start. Students who are new to model diplomacy can quickly feel overwhelmed by the magnitude of what they are being asked to undertake. The challenge of stepping into the shoes of a diplomat to represent a country on a committee with highly specialized topics is intimidating and, to many, a seemingly impossible task. The academic conference where they will square off against students from other schools in a public setting adds a daunting element to the challenge, the temptation to drop out of the class or club is great. There are differences of opinion of how to get things started. To some, it is best to throw the students into the fire to quickly see which have the determination and courage to stay with the program beyond the first week. Separating the wheat from the chaff accordingly, narrows the group to the students who can best represent the school at the conference. I take issue with the 'sink or swim' philosophy for several reasons. From my decades in the classroom, I've found that many students are reticent to step out of their comfort zone and risk failure, especially if a grade is on the line. Model diplomacy, if nothing else, is an exercise in stepping out of comfort zones. It requires a wide range of skills that few students possess on the first day of class. Public speaking, debate, document drafting and research are essential elements that are developed over time. If some students are particularly strong in two or three areas, the delegation still needs students who excel in the other areas. Only accepting students who are "conference ready" at the onset deprives the delegation of those who can contribute to the overall quality of the group. Further, the purpose of education at all levels is to cumulatively build knowledge, skills and experience for students who enter the classroom with differing degrees of maturity, experience and interest. Some of the most successful students in my program have been those who, from their own account, felt least prepared for the challenge at the onset. Finally, and most importantly, the measure of success of a model diplomacy program is not performance at the conference. Rather, it is the long-term impact that the experience has on the students who participate. If their diplomacy experience makes them more aware of the complicated international environment and the skills that they develop enhance their professional preparedness, the program was a success for them. For these reasons, I suggest an inclusive approach to building the team.

Begin the first meeting with a basic overview of the conference trip, briefly explaining what the students will encounter from opening to closing ceremonies. Highlight the free time to explore the host city and note the days and times of the conference sessions. To engage the students, each is asked to come to the podium and deliver a short pre-drafted speech, which reads:

> "Fellow delegates, my name is _____ . When I graduate I hope to _____."

Before the students return to their seat, they are provided with a research binder. When all speeches are delivered, ask the students to take out their name placards and position them (tent style) in front of them. Explain that at conference, they will have a country placard that will be required to make motions and vote. Require them to bring their placards to each session and to raise the placard if they would like to speak, make a comment or to ask a question. Refuse to recognize a student until they have raised their placard and allow them to speak once they are formally recognized by the chair.

Your goal in this first meeting of the group is to excite the students about the challenge ahead, provide them with confidence that they will be successful in meeting the challenge and to insure them that, as a group, they will be an impressive delegation. Provide the students with the six principles of a successful program, as outlined below.

Principle 1. Egalitarian. Everyone enters the training protocol on an equal footing. Differences of background, maturity, personality and style do not separate the delegation into groups that determine their role in the program. I am fortunate that all of the students in my diplomacy classes are first timers to model United Nations. There are programs that allow returning students to take the class again the following year for academic credit, creating a two-tiered delegation based on experience. Often in these situations, a veteran model diplomacy student is paired with a student who is new to the class and has not participated in a conference. The new student plays a support role and follows the lead of the experienced student. I do not subscribe to this approach, recognizing that many students will have only one opportunity to participate in a diplomacy conference and, therefore, should make the most of it.

Principle 2. Unitary. Teamwork is an essential element of the success of any model diplomacy delegation. For most schools, which are assigned to represent one country at the conference, it is much easier to promote solidarity of the mission. With large delegations, multiple states must be assigned to accommodate all the students. My program has represented as many as eight countries in a conference, which effectively pits students against each other for favor among the conference judges. I stress the need to work together, show support for each other and the sharing of information across country assignments for the greater good. If your group is so large that you will need to request multiple country assignments, consider at the time of conference registration if you prefer to select nation-states with similar interests (Belgium, Netherlands) or those who are not traditional negotiating partners (Iran, Canada).

Principle 3. Progressive. It is very easy for students to feel overwhelmed by the magnitude of the challenge that lies ahead. They must quickly learn a multitude of aspects of their assigned country, learn background information about their committee topics, determine their country's position on the topics and come up with an angle to address the topics that is novel and promotable to most committee delegates. Additionally, the students must sharpen their public speaking and debate skills and learn how to draft formal documents, or resolutions, at the conference. The progressive approach outlined in this manual takes the students on a step-by-step preparation plan to acquire the knowledge and skills required for success. To lower the likelihood of students feeling overwhelmed, I limit the announcement of future assignments to a few weeks. There is no benefit in the first few week of class to introduce the students to position papers as the deadline for most conferences will be mid-way through the semester. Convincing the students that they will reach the apex of preparation through a series of small and manageable steps is key to keeping them on board and moving in the right direction.

Principle 4. Adaptability. It is said that the first casualty in war is the game plan. In model diplomacy, the game plan outlined in this manual is never sacrificed due to changing circumstances, but modifications on the way to the conference will always be required. Students drop out for a variety of reasons, the world that they are studying changes dramatically and without warning, and weather-related events can upset the schedule. Teaching in South Florida brings with it the prospect of losing a week or longer to major hurricanes in the run up to the November conference. Students must be resilient and ready to adapt to changing circumstances. The most severe example of adaptability occurred in my program twenty years ago at a Midwest conference. We traveled with ten students who were assigned to six committees, with doubling up allowed. As such, eight students were paired with partners and two students represented their country without a committee partner. At the start of the first session, we learned of a structural issue affecting one of the committee rooms, making it no longer usable by the conference. This forced the organizers to move UNICEF to another location. Because the new room was smaller, it could not accommodate all the students who had been assigned to the committee. I had no choice but to ask one student, who had diligently prepared for UNICEF and its two topics, to instead represent her country in the General Assembly with a classmate who had expected to be alone. All that I could do was to remind the student that she was well trained in diplomatic skills and knowledgeable about her assigned country and to do her best to excel. Adaptability and flexibility are key components of success.

Principle 5. Focus. Of the principles outlined in this section, number five—FOCUS—is the most challenging for students of all ages. While they are often sharp and attentive under direct supervision and in the fulfillment of a specific assignment, they are quick to let their guards down and lapse in concentration at times. I remind my students that they can perform perfectly for a three-hour session at the conference, only to undermine their status in the eyes of the judges if they lose focus and appear unprofessional for even an instance. The best time to remind the students to FOCUS is when they are transitioning from one activity to another.

Principle 6. Professionalism. The goal of secondary and post-secondary education is much more than teaching concepts, information and analytic skills. Additionally, we are preparing young people to confront a highly competitive world. Acting in a professional manner is a learned skill and there is no better setting to teach it than in model diplomacy preparation.

Conclude the review of program principles by introducing the Golden Rule, which is borrowed from Sir Isaac Newton:

A Body in Motion Tends to Stay in Motion,
a Body at Rest Tends to Stay at Rest.

The typical student will feel slightly overwhelmed by the early simulations and often wrongly assumes that others in the class are better prepared to lead the negotiations and make speeches. As a result, they decide to hold back and let others go first. Before they know it, the simulation is concluding, and their participation has been minimal if not non-existent. No matter their personality or disposition, it is imperative that they jump in from the start and participate. As we say in my program, week one mistakes are expected, making them a month into preparation is not. Making mistakes early is the first step to success later, learning from those mistakes is the essential second step. I discourage teaming students together for most classroom simulations because more often than not the less confident student will follow the other, delaying their development.

At this point, you have completed your first meeting of the semester. The students feel a combination of excitement, nervousness, and trepidation. It is important to tell them that this mix of feelings is normal and expected, and that you have full confidence that the class will be fully prepared by the time the conference rolls around. In the next session, whether it is after a ten-minute break for two-hour meetings or days later for split classes, students take on their first simulation. Since no advanced information about the simulation is provided, it is important to close the session with assignments (short speeches, geography quiz) for the following few weeks.

In week number two, short speeches are delivered. The presentations are sixty seconds in length and cover a single topic relating to the assigned country. One topic, such as those listed below, is assigned to each student.

If your group is representing more than one country, have a representative from each country deliver a speech on the same topic.

Geography	Government	Economy
Capital	Flag	Resources
Religion	Educational System	Ethnicity
UN Membership	Independence	Border States

The only directions that should be provided to the students are that the speech pertains to their assigned country and the sixty-second time limit. It is important not to provide any additional information about sources, format or delivery. Part of the assignment is for students to figure out the best way to prepare and deliver a speech. Some will memorize the speech; others will use a print copy. Many will use flashcards, but most will type the speech into their phones to read aloud. There is no wrong way to deliver the speech, but there certainly is a right way, a diplomatic way, to do so. In week 2A, you will listen to the presentations and then instruct the students how to properly deliver a diplomatic speech moving forward.

In weeks two through five, regional geography quizzes are assigned. Requiring students to possess a cursory knowledge of country locations serves several purposes. While their preparation attention is directed towards their assigned country, during in-class simulations and at the conference they will interact with nation-states from across the globe. At the United Nations regional groupings form natural caucus partnerships, a tendency that is replicated at model diplomacy conferences. I divide the world into four regions (Latin America, Asia, Africa, Europe) and instruct the students to be prepared to identify countries in each region. For each quiz, provide a map of the region being tested and randomly label ten countries. Students then identify the country to complete the quiz. Some instructors quiz students on geographic features (bodies of water, mountains, etc.), I prefer to ask my students to focus on country locations. An additional benefit of assignment geography quizzes is that they are easy ways for students to earn points. Successful completion of a geography quiz builds their confidence that they are making progress towards conference preparation.

Week 1B

The First Simulation

The class begins, like all others for the remainder of the semester, with roll call. When the student's name is called, they are to raise their placards and respond with PRESENT. Distribute the simulation below and pound the gavel to commence the first simulation.

A Matter of Urgent Importance

Two sides have agreed upon a meeting between their heads of state. An isolated nation has been chosen to host the summit. The centuries-old building where the leaders and their support staff will negotiate has two levels. The summit will be held on the main level and the basement is partitioned, with each nation's negotiation staff splitting the space. On the lower level there are two bathrooms, with each side wanting the larger one. The host, not expecting a standoff over the facilities, has left it to the two sides to determine how to allocate the bathrooms.

PARTIES: The United States of America and the Union of Soviet Socialist Republics.

CHALLENGE: Determine the allocation of the lower-level bathrooms.

TIME LIMIT: 30 minutes.

Prep Material. None. Divide the class evenly between the USA and USSR.

Directions for the Chair. This initial simulation does not require placards as rules of parliamentary procedure have not yet been introduced and are not used in this exercise. Announce to the students that they have fifteen minutes to discuss the issue, after which speeches will be allowed. Once speeches are delivered, announce a ten-minute caucus for final negotiations before a vote is taken. With only two participants, both must agree on a proposed settlement. Invite one delegation (USA, USSR) to make a proposal, followed by a vote. If the two sides agree, the simulation has successfully been completed. If not, invite the other delegation to make a proposal. Continue until a settlement is reached.

Recap. This is an excellent first simulation for students who are new to model diplomacy and the negotiated settlement of disputes. It is simple in that there are only two actors, with students evenly divided into teams. The issue in dispute, how to allocate bathroom space, creates levity and is relatable to all participants. At the same time, the matter must be addressed and a resolution reached.

After the simulation is concluded and a decision reached by the participants, the chair should make two points. First, explain the standard process of negotiation. Normally, the two parties stake out an extreme position to start the session seeking to satisfy their narrow interest with little regard to the interests of the other. In this simulation, for example, the United States may propose to have exclusive rights to the larger bathroom. Such a position is untenable and is countered by a Soviet proposal to allow its delegation to have the larger bathroom. Once the extremes are eliminated, the two sides begin to inch towards the center of the spectrum where an agreement can be reached.

When diplomatic negotiations satisfy some, but not all, of each party's preferences, a compromise can be reached. Second, it is important to instruct them that the starting point of any negotiation is a listing of possible options.

Common proposals, with the most extreme at the beginning and end of the list:

1. Team A is allowed to use the larger restroom,
2. Gender-based allocation of the restrooms,
3. The bathrooms are open to all representatives of the two teams,
4. Set schedule of hours for the use of each bathroom by the respective teams, and
5. Team B is allowed to use the larger restroom.

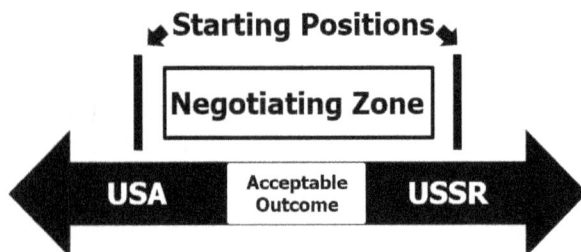

Starting Positions

Negotiating Zone

USA   Acceptable Outcome   USSR

This simulation, which appears simplistic and manufactured, has its place in history. In the 1980s, American President Ronald Reagan and Soviet Premier Michael Gorbachev agreed to hold a summit to discuss nuclear weapons. They chose Reykjavik, Iceland, as the meeting place for the summit. The advance teams for each superpower arrived early to set the protocol for the summit and negotiate space allocation in the building. Confronting the dilemma over two bathrooms of differing size, they decided that any member of the respective delegations could use either bathroom during the negotiations. The summit ended in failure, as the heads of state were not able to agree upon nuclear arms reductions, however, the meeting is credited with setting the stage for the conclusion of the Intermediate-Range Nuclear Force (INF) Treaty in 1987.

Week 2A

The Diplomatic Speech

Begin the class with roll call. Inform the students that when their name is called, they are to raise their placards and respond with the formal name of their assigned country (i.e., The Republic of the Congo is present). Administer the regional geography quiz and, when concluded, remind the students which region will be the subject of the next week's quiz. By week number two your delegation should be firmly in place as any who have decided not to continue likely made that decision by now. Student travel normally requires paperwork submitted well in advance of the travel dates. Week two is a good time to start collecting the required information for submission. This is also the time to announce committee assignments. Students learned of their country assignment in the first week, it is now time to match them up with partners and assign them to a committee. Some teachers allow students to self-select, others match veteran students with new ones. I randomly match students without regard to background, major or personality. After more than thirty years assigning committee partners, I don't think that it is possible to know early in the training protocol how to effectively assign partners.

Formal speechmaking is the key skill taught in week two. Call the students in random order to deliver their assigned 60-second topic speech that was assigned the previous week. When the class has completed the assignment, it is time to instruct them on the proper way to deliver a model diplomacy speech. They need to understand that public speaking is a challenge for most people. In the United States, Glossophobia—the fear of public speaking—is a recognized condition and is considered a type of social anxiety disorder. It is also widespread. When asked, respondents list public speaking as their number one fear with death ranking number three. Rather than emphasizing the negative aspects of public speaking, highlight the fact that once they have mastered public speaking they will have a significant advantage over most people. Assure them that within a few weeks, with the information that you are about to provide, they will be well on their way to becoming accomplished public speakers.

Angle. All speeches, formal and informal, fall into one of four categories as illustrated below.

	Outside	Inside
Objective	Academic Speech	
Subjective		Diplomatic Speech

An "Outside" speech is one that considers the topic (country flag, capital, population, etc.) from afar. It contains words such as "their government" or "its resources." When delivered in an objective fashion, we have the classic academic speech. The presentation outlines the good, the bad and the ugly of the country to provide a wholistic understanding of the topic. An "Inside" speech is one where the presenter is speaking on behalf of the nation. Diplomats, as government-appointed representatives, are tasked with giving an international voice to her or his fellow citizens. Diplomatic speeches are not objective, rather they focus on the positive and downplay, if not outright disregard, the negative. A large part of the diplomat's profile is that of a public relations officer. An "Inside-Subjective" speech reflects what the government wants the world to hear. There is no situation where a diplomat cannot put enough "spin" on a speech to put their government in a favorable light.

Typical Phrases For Each Type of Speech	
Outside-Objective	Inside-Subjective
That country The population Their	My country Our population We
The cold, hard truth about the country.	A sanitized version of the truth.

All speeches from this point forward are to be written and delivered as Inside-Subjective presentations, reflecting the interests of the assigned country.

Materials. At the model diplomacy conference, speeches are made during formal sessions. Either by raising their placard or through an online portal, student-delegates place their country name on the speakers' list. When it is their turn, the delegate proceeds to the podium to deliver a prepared speech. There will be a time limit, generally 30- or 60-seconds. Students should be aware that the speaking time may be altered by a motion that is supported by a majority of voting delegates.

The materials brought to the podium to deliver a speech are important and impacting on the overall quality of the presentation. The options include:

No Materials for a Memorized Speech
Flashcards
Bullet Points
Cell Phone
Computer
Handwritten Speech
Printed Typed Speech

It is highly discouraged to allow students to opt for one of the first three (memorized, flashcards, bullet points) approaches. Speeches that are memorized can go sideways very quickly when the person making the delivery loses their train of thought. This is more likely to happen when they are taken out of their element, such as delivering a speech in a large room with 200 sets of eyes on them. Flashcards are problematic when they are inadvertently placed in the wrong order, which can happen if their nerves get the better of them and they drop the cards on the way to the podium. No one wants to have hundreds of fellow delegates watch them pick up and reorder their flashcards while the clock on their speech is ticking. Speeches given using bullet points can be successful; however, they are more likely to be less formal as the student mentally decides on how to frame each bullet point and transition from one to the next.

I allow each student to determine what remaining material (cell phone, computer, handwritten, print) they will use to deliver their speeches, but warn them of the dangers of the first two especially. I have countless times seen cell phones and computers begin a software update just as the delegate approaches the podium. Further, cell phones and computers use batteries, which tend to die at the most inopportune time. Without question, the safest and most effective strategy in delivering a speech is the printed version. The advantages include:

No Batteries or Updates
Audience/Dias/Judges See That the Student is Prepared
Easily Revised as Needed
A Place to Put Both Hands During the Speech

Making eye contact during the speech adds a positive element to the delivery. I advise students to pre-select the two or three places in the speech when their eyes will leave the drafted document to make eye contact and to use a yellow highlighter to mark the next word to help them correctly return their focus on the paper. This allows them to seamlessly deliver the speech without losing their spot after making eye contact. Every speech given during the training simulations must be drafted, whether handwritten or on a cell phone, and at no time is a student allowed to deliver an impromptu or memorized speech. By the time your delegation arrives at the conference, delivering prepared speeches will be the norm.

Purpose. Delivering a high-quality speech is only part of the consideration. Why speeches are given, in general and at a model diplomacy conference, is important as well. There are four reasons for delivering a speech, some more reflective of a diplomat's mission than others. When asked why a speech is given, the go-to response is "To provide information." Without question, the answer is correct. However, the provision of information is secondary to the other three purposes of a diplomatic speech. The second reason to give a speech is to draw attention to one aspect of a topic. A third purpose is to persuade other student-delegates to think about an issue or your assigned country in a way that reflects the government's interests or policy position. In other words, persuasion. Finally, and often undervalued, is the goal of impressing the audience with a quality speech delivered professionally. Formal session is the only time that a delegate can monopolize the attention of the committee, it is imperative that they make the most of the opportunity. In large committees, students may only have the opportunity to make two or three speeches during the course of the conference. If you are doubling up on committee assignments, that could mean that each of your students makes only one speech. When a model diplomacy delegate steps to the podium to make a formal speech, all eyes are on them and they are being judged. Delivering a quality speech translates into positive perceptions and an increased likelihood that other delegates will seek them out during informal sessions to work together.

Speech Sections. To deliver quality speeches, students must abide by an established structure in the drafting of their message. There are three sections of a speech: Open, Body, Close. The **Open** is a simple and straightforward four-word phrase, "Honorable Chair, Fellow Delegates." There are two reasons for the Open. The first is that it is standard protocol. Diplomats adhere to an unwritten code of conduct that is uniform across the community of nations that dictates how they interact in all sorts of situations. I've had coffee with representatives from the Islamic Republic of Iran and the Swiss Confederation. You could not find two more opposite nation-states, yet their diplomats interact in remarkably similar fashion. Beginning every speech with the stated Open is the norm and all students should adopt it. Inform your students that every speech in class is required to begin with the Diplomatic Open. The second reason for the Open is to get the ball rolling. Students will be nervous as they approach the podium for the first (or tenth) time with all eyes upon them. Having delivered the standard Diplomatic Open dozens of times in class will allow them a comfortable segue into the body of the speech. Before the Open, however, the student should be stationary with feet and shoulders square and chin directed at the microphone. A "Walking Open" is one where the student begins the speech before fully arriving at the podium. Looking back to the dais when delivering the Open creates a break with the microphone that should be avoided.

The second section of the formal speech is the **Body**, which encompasses all that the delegate wishes to convey to the committee. It should be noted that people's attention spans are not generally very long, model diplomacy conferences are no exception. Students sitting in their seats are tired, excited, nervous and/or focusing on the speech that they are planning to deliver. As a result, the student making the formal speech has their full attention often only at the beginning and end of the presentation. For that reason, it is imperative that the country name is mentioned in the first three seconds of the speech. I suggest the full, formal name of the country (i.e., The United Kingdom of Great Britain and Northern Ireland as opposed to the United Kingdom or the U.K.). The name of the country should be included in the final sentence of the speech, as well as at least two additional times during the speech. From this point forward, every prepared speech in class must include the country's name a minimum of three times. The final part of the speech is the **Close**, which is "Thank

You." A "walking close" is delivered as the student is in motion to return to their seat and should be avoided.

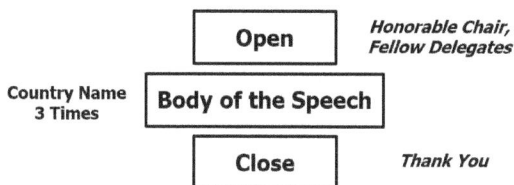

Open	*Honorable Chair, Fellow Delegates*
Body of the Speech	*Country Name 3 Times* (left)
Close	*Thank You*

The keys to training your students to deliver impressive diplomatic speeches are repetition and regulation. Repetition relates to how often they practice giving speeches, both during simulations and during assignments. Regulation is the responsibility of the instructor or group leader to track each speech, using the chart provided below, and communicating to each student where their speech is lacking. I require the open, country name (3 times) and close, along with proper posture, tempo and volume for every speech delivered after the second week. Allowing them to slack on any of the required components of a speech builds in bad habits that become increasingly difficult to correct as the semester unfolds. For all speeches delivered in class, assigned and during a simulation, use the metric below to track individual and overall conformity with the proper structure and delivery.

Charting formal speeches.

Student	Open	Country Name	Tempo	Volume	Posture	Close	Comments
Randy	+	IIII	fast	proper	Feet/shoulders	+	

Remind the students that the next geography quiz is given in week three. Inform the students that they are only responsible for nation-states, not territories, and only required to know where each country is located on a blank map. Dismiss the class, reminding them to bring their name placards to each session.

Week 2B

Simulation: Fatal Decision

A group of people is on a life raft with limited food and water. For the others to survive, one person must be thrown overboard.

PARTICIPANTS:

Priest, male, age 61
Doctor, female, age 49
Chemist, female, age 52
Child, male, age 11
Housewife and mother of three, female, age 33
Navy engineer, uncertain gender, age 23
Senior citizen, female, age 71
Nurse, male, age 40

The fatal decision is a formal statement that selects one of the members to be thrown overboard that is supported by all participants. Any decision not to decide or a failure to reach agreement on a joint statement will endanger all members of the raft and will constitute a failed simulation.

Robert's rules of parliamentary procedure will be used. Students may make a motion to enter into informal caucus at any time for a maximum of ten minutes. Delegates wishing to speak must be placed on the speakers' list and wait to be recognized by the chair. Speeches are limited to 30 seconds.

Time Limit: 45 minutes

Prep Material. None.

Directions for the Chair. It is now time to begin to introduce Robert's Rules of Order. Some instructors emphasize the rules, teach them to the students and quiz them on their competence. I do not share this strategy. While there are seventeen key rules of order utilized in model diplomacy, only a few are needed much of the time. Additionally, any competent simulation chair will explain the implications and requirements of a motion when it is raised by a delegate, making memorizing and drilling students on the rules of parliamentary procedure an unnecessary commitment of time and energy. One of the most common motions is to break into informal session, or caucus. After being recognized by the Chair, the student-delegate should stand and state: "Honorable Chair, the Dominion of Canada moves for a suspension of the meeting for the purpose of caucus for a period of ten minutes." If the motion is seconded and receives a majority of votes it is adopted and the committee moves into informal session for the allotted time. During caucus sessions, students may move around the room to negotiate with other delegates.

After gaveling the session into order, announce that the speakers' list is open and ask for a show of placards of those who wish to be placed on the list. Once that is complete, invite a motion to caucus—guiding students through the process is more helpful than simply stating "The floor is open to motions." Announce the end of the caucus session when time expires and work through the speakers' list until it is exhausted. Then invite a motion to caucus to allow further discussion, followed by speeches. When you feel that the students are ready to vote, invite a motion to select a member of the boat to be selected. A student should rise to their feet, as they always do when making a procedural motion, and identify an individual to be sacrificed. Notify the students that they may vote YES or NO and take a vote by show of placards. If there are no dissenting votes, the session ends. If there is a NO vote, inform them that the proposal is not adopted and ask for other motions to select an individual. I do not allow a reconsideration of a selection that was voted down previously because motions to reconsider are cumbersome and usually not understood by students new to model diplomacy. Normally, the students will realize quickly that they all need to vote YES to complete the simulation and receive full credit for their effort.

Recap. Life-boat ethics is a classic simulation. Students represent themselves and must make a collective choice among unpleasant options. It is important to stress that there are no wrong answers and that any member of the group could logically be selected to go overboard. To succeed, however, the students must unanimously agree on which passenger is selected. Since unanimity is the requirement, power is located on the fringes as any delegate's disagreeing vote will doom all the passengers and result in a failed simulation. The class tends to divide into like-minded groups (LMGs) with the largest, from my experience using this simulation for three decades, is the 71-year old female senior citizen. Students lean towards that choice with the logic that she can offer the group less than the others. A second, smaller group of student-delegates usually gravitates towards the Navy engineer, using the argument that s/he has the best chance of surviving if thrown overboard. In 1998, one of my students insisted on selecting the 11-year-old child and refused to compromise. From her Native American culture, a person's value to the community is measured by their life experience. As such, all other people on the raft offered more life experience than the child. That was one of the few times that the class failed to select a person and, therefore, did not successfully complete the assignment.

The primary purpose of this simulation is to understand the dynamic of Principle v. Process. The principle is the issue to be decided, in this case the selection of one member of the boat crew to throw overboard. The process refers to parameters. For this simulation the parameters are a formal decision that is adopted unanimously within the allotted time. If student-delegates overly focus on the principle, attempting to find the perfect answer among imperfect options, they lose sight of the time limit and risk not finishing on time. If the students singularly focus on the process, they will move to adopt a decision without adequately debating the principle. The record completion time for my classes is eleven minutes. I explained to the students that while they completed the task, judges would not reward their lack of debate, negotiation and speeches. Every simulation, regardless of the principle at hand or the process requirements, requires a balance between the two for optimal results. Multitasking (listening to the speeches of others, drafting documents, passing diplomatic notes, negotiating) is a key component of any successful simulation, time management is of equal importance.

Week 3A

Position Papers

After roll call and the geography quiz, week three is the time to introduce students to the position paper. Position papers are a mainstay at academic conferences, sometimes for social conferences and almost never for fantasy models. There are several purposes of position papers. First, they provide each committee member with the opportunity to formally state their position on each of the assigned topics. Second, when the papers are posted in the weeks leading up to the conference, they communicate the views of member-states in a public space. Finally, position papers are often judged for separate awards.

The position paper is a two-page document that covers both (or all) committee topics. The first aspect of the paper to address is format. If the position paper is improperly drafted, it signals a lack of precision, if not seriousness, about the committee's business and the preparation of the delegation. To assist students in properly drafting the position paper, I provide the following checklist.

Formatting the Position Paper

_____ Confirm that you reviewed the Position Paper document found at nmun.org

_____ Length of 2 pages _____ 1" margins _____ Font Arial Size 10

_____ Title: center, bold "Delegation From…"

_____ Center bold & italics: "Position Paper for (insert Committee)"

_____ Double-space between "Position Paper for…" and first paragraph

_____ First paragraph: "The topics before the (Committee) are…"

_____ 2nd sentence: "The (official country name) looks forward to…."

_____ Double-space after 1st paragraph

_____ Center, bold Roman numeral I: title of topic #1

_____ Double-space after topic I title

_____ 1st paragraph for topic I: three full sentences about the importance of the topic

_____ Double-space after 1st paragraph

_____ 2nd paragraph for topic I full paragraph referencing at least three UN or int'l docs

_____ Double-space after 2nd paragraph

_____ 3rd paragraph for topic I full paragraph describing how to resolve the challenge

_____ Double-space after 3rd paragraph

_____ Center, bold Roman numeral II: title of topic #2

Follow the same format for Topic number two and others, if applicable.

_____ Use full citation of documents: A/RES/70/1 should read as General Assembly resolution 70/1 (2018)

_____ When using an acronym, provide full name followed by acronym in ()

_____ example: the United Nations (UN) or General Assembly (GA) 2nd

_____ For all future references to the above, only us the acronym (i.e., UN)

For Submission of the Position Paper

_____ Document saved using this model: COMMITTEE_COUNTRY (ECOSOC_Canada)

Knowing how to format a position paper is only part of the drafting process. Students must conduct research to ensure that their paper accurately reflects the policy position of their assigned country, demonstrates an understanding of the topics and promotes a viable resolution of the challenge. If your conference provides a background guide, that is the best place to start. Students should also consult reputable sources for United Nations documents, international agreements and scholarly analyses that are on point.

Introducing the position paper assignment in week three gives ample time for students to conduct the necessary research and complete drafting of the document prior to the conference deadline. I suggest that you establish a rough draft deadline approximately one week before the final submission is due for an initial review. Some schools place a premium on the drafting of position papers and are often acknowledged with awards at the conference for their commitment. They spend large amounts of class time reviewing and revising the documents and use multiple draft deadlines for honing the papers to perfection.

The position paper is composed of three paragraphs per topic. The first paragraph explains the importance of the topic and identifies which aspects the country contends are most important. The second paragraph references the relevant international work that has been completed, in whole or in part, to address the topic. Important here are documents adopted by international organizations, treaties reached by nation-states and documents released by relevant bodies. The third paragraph outlines ideas and suggestions for remediating the issue. A sample position paper for one topic is provided below.

Delegation from the Republic of Poland
Position Paper for the Human Rights Council

The topics before the Human Rights Council (HRC) are Access to Safe Drinking Water as a Fundamental Human Right and Preventing Discrimination and Violence Against Persons with Disabilities. The Republic of Poland recognizes the need for strong international cooperation to monitor and implement access to vital human rights, and it looks forward to discussing these topics at the upcoming conference.

1. Access to Safe Drinking Water as a Fundamental Human Right

According to the United Nations (UN) World Health Organization (WHO), over 1 billion people throughout the world lack access to clean drinking water. WHO and the UN Children's Fund's (UNICEF) Joint Monitoring Programme (JMP) for Water Supply and Sanitation has stated that the water that 1.8 billion people drink exhibits fecal contamination. The deprivation of the fundamental right to safe drinking water particularly afflicts the most marginalized members of global society, including women, displaced persons, persons with disabilities, the impoverished, and children. Those without access to safe drinking water often also suffer from economic and social disadvantages, including medical conditions, lack of access to education, and lack of employment. The Republic of Poland is dedicated to aiding Member States and to improving infrastructure for the promotion and protection of the right to safe drinking water.

Access to safe drinking water as a basic human right has been discussed extensively on the international level. While the foundational *Universal Declaration of Human Rights* (UDHR) of 1948 does not explicitly discuss water, it established "the right to life, liberty and security of persons" and the right to "a standard of living adequate for the health and well-being" of individuals. In 1977, the *Mar del Plata Action Plan* from the UN Water Conference held in Argentina first recognized water as a human right. In 2010, the UN General Assembly (GA) acknowledged the human right to water in resolution 64/292, which also discussed the connection between access to safe drinking water and the achievement of all other human rights. The Sustainable Development Goals (SDGs) include SDG 6 on clean water and sanitation. Poland supports HRC resolution 15/9, which stressed the importance of Member State support of human rights programs pertaining to access to safe drinking water. Poland also applauds the adoption of HRC resolution 18/1, which called for transparency, diligent analysis, and prioritized action for populations most in need. Poland upholds the continued work of the Special Rapporteur on the human right to safe drinking water and sanitation, as well as the UN Inter-Agency Mechanism on all Freshwater Related Issues, Including Sanitation (UN-Water). Regionally, the European Union (EU) has emphasized that effective water management is important for all EU countries. Nationally, Poland is proud of the work within its own borders and throughout the world by its government and non-governmental organizations (NGOs). Poland is a country considered to have less available in-country water resources than many other European countries; however, 99% of urban citizens and nearly 97% of rural citizens have access to an improved drinking water source. In Poland, a minister has been appointed to consider issues related to water management, and in June 2015, Poland hosted a National Water Forum to discuss access to water in Poland, which encouraged the sharing of ideas through public consultations towards updated Water Management Plans. At the UN Sustainable Development Summit in September 2015, Andrzej Duda, the President of Poland, emphasized the continued need of the international community to address access to water.

Poland stresses the need for Member States to lead and coordinate efforts to help developing countries. As such, Poland recommends the international implementation of measures proposed by the Special Rapporteur. These proposals would require legislative and social changes within individual Member States and should contain legal consequences for discriminatory practices in water distribution and access in regards to a person's ethnicity, nationality, gender, or social status. Other considerations should include support such as food aid, medical assistance, and access to water sources. Furthermore, additional changes should include increased support by NGOs, national governments, and the international community for community infrastructures such as plumbing fixtures and water connections. It is important that voluntary financial support is made available to assist Member States in improving drinking water infrastructure in order to ensure that all have access to it. As such practices are implemented, more communities will obtain a higher standard of living through access to safe drinking water, and the human rights of global citizens can be more fully realized.

*Source: NMUN.ORG

The remaining time in Week 3A can be filled with an exercise that helps the students develop their impromptu speaking skills and provides a series of teaching moments for the delegation. I call this exercise, which is an excellent time filler at any segment of the training protocol, "What Would You Do?" Call on students one at a time to come to the front of the class. Inform them that they will be placed in a specific scenario and ask them to briefly respond by stating what they would do. The students are required to use their open (Honorable Chair, Fellow Delegates) and close (Thank You) to re-enforce the structure of all speeches. Below is a sample list of questions that I use, each is followed by an explanation of what students should do at the conference if they find themselves in a similar situation. I note to the class that each of the scenarios is taken from an experience by a past fellow delegate in the program. After each of the questions listed below, I provide the reader with how I use the situation as a teaching opportunity. Some of the scenarios discussed below are reviewed in more detail in the chapter titled At the Conference. My full list of What Would You Do questions totals more than thirty scenarios; therefore the "game" is played out over several class A sessions until all students have had the opportunity to respond and all scenarios are covered.

Sample What Would You Do Questions & Debriefs

Question: You wake up on the day of departure and have the flu.

Debrief: Remind the students that life often gets in the way of the most well-made plans. People get sick at the most inopportune time and falling ill may prevent a student from attending the conference. Sickness during the conference is not out of the question either. Regardless, students should be informed that failing to attend or fully participate in the conference proceedings for reasons not their own is not their fault and will not be held against them. Safety is the priority of every team leader, including the well-being of the people who travel with or share a hotel room with a sick person. This is also a chance to remind the students that while they each have a committee partner, their partner may not always be in session and they must be ready (remind them of the Adaptable principle from class 1A) to represent their county alone.

Question: You miss your flight.

Debrief: Whether you are traveling with secondary or post-secondary students, many have not experienced a missed flight and do not know what to do if it happens to them. Some assume that they will be required to purchase a ticket on another flight. Explain the process of reporting to the airline desk and requesting to be placed on the next available flight to the conference city. They should also understand the importance of communicating with the group leader about their status and expected time of arrival.

Question: You feel overwhelmed and intimidated at the first session.

Debrief: Assure the students that this is completely normal and expected. They have been training together and have experienced simulation sessions where a pattern of working together for the common good has been developed. When they arrive at the conference, everything is different. There are more people on the committee, many of whom have attended model diplomacy conferences in the past and some are not interested in working toward the common good. The conference environment can be incredibly intimidating for first-time students. Remind them that they have been well trained and that their mission is not to dominate the session but to find a small number of delegates to work with on their common document. This is a good time to ask them to repeat the Golden Rule that was introduced in week one and encourage them to jump in and start working with others.

Question: A student from another university attempts to dominate the first caucus.

Debrief: Model diplomacy conferences bring together a motley crew of students with differing backgrounds, interests, professional intentions and personalities. Some view the conference as a zero-sum game where they can only win at the expense of other delegates. Others hide their insecurity or lack of preparation behind extreme levels of confidence. The proper response to a domineering delegate is to break away with a few others and form a caucus group to begin drafting a working paper or resolution.

Question: Someone steals your idea for a resolution.

Debrief: First of all, just because someone has the same idea for a resolution does not mean that they have stolen yours. They may have thought of it at the same time or even before you came up with it. The student has two options: either work with the other student on the common idea or find a new idea to draft a resolution about.

Question: You're next on the speakers' list & the student ahead of you delivers a speech that mirrors the one you prepared.

Debrief: With a large number of student-delegates delivering speeches on the same topic, inevitably there will be an overlap of material. Most students will respond that they would rewrite their speech on the way to the podium. This violates the prohibition on impromptu speeches and never works in the student's favor. Instead, remind them that the attention span of students, like most people, is very short. Delegates are judged by their peers more for delivery and style than substance. Therefore, they should go to the podium and deliver their prepared speech without concern about the overlap as few will actually notice.

Question: One of your fellow delegates just collapsed.

Debrief: Dial 9-1-1. It is difficult to recall the number of medical emergencies that I have witnessed over the decades. Students get so bound up in their committee work, and fun after session, that they fail to properly nourish and hydrate. This is an opportunity to remind them to take care of themselves and to keep an eye out for each other.

Question: You are cozy in bed and decide that you want to get ice from the hotel ice machine.

Debrief: Years ago, a student did exactly this, forgetting that a conference hotel with 3,000 college students can create situations that are not safe. In the hallway, he stepped on a piece of glass and spent the evening in an emergency room for stitches. He spent the remainder of the conference in bed with his foot elevated. You can never drive home the safety issue enough with students.

At the conclusion of class, inform the students that their first formal speech (Agenda Setting) is due in two weeks. Each delegate must draft a 60-second speech to set the agenda order (i.e., Topic 1 followed by Topic 2 or Topic 2 followed by Topic 1). Provide them with no additional information except for them to prepare the speech as they best see fit. More information about the agenda speech and how it is to be drafted is provided at the appropriate time in this prep guide.

Week 3B

Simulation: City Selection

The World Economic Forum (WEF) selected five cities as finalists to host the annual gathering of world leaders and industry elites. The meeting today is scheduled to select the host city.

The finalists are Berlin, Tokyo, Rio, Casablanca and Warsaw.

PARTICIPANTS: Nation-states from across the international system.

Through a series of voting rounds, states will have the option of casting a 'favorable' vote for each of the finalist cities. States can vote in favor of any, all or none of the cities. The city receiving the lowest number of votes will be eliminated after each round of voting.

Select a finalist city to host the World Economic Forum.

Time Limit: 60 minutes.

Vote Tabulation Table (example)

	Round 1	Round 2	Round 3	Round 4	Round 5
Berlin	17	16	16	16	X
Tokyo	14	15	17	19	Selected
Rio	8	8	X	X	X
Casablanca	11	11	9	X	X
Warsaw	7	X	X	X	X

Prep Material. Placards for Germany, Japan, Brazil, Morocco and Poland, plus enough other countries (regionally balanced) for each student.

Directions for the Chair. Randomly assign each student with a placard. The country assignments should be roughly balanced between the five regions represented in the competing cities (Western Europe, Eastern Europe, Asia, Africa, Latin America). Gavel the session to order, open the speakers' list and invite a motion to caucus. By now the students will be familiar with the rhythm of the simulations. You will want to limit caucus sessions to ten minutes before returning to formal sessions for speeches. Students representing the five cities bidding to host the Forum should naturally understand that they want to win the competition and be awarded the host city designation. This is not always the case but should not be corrected by the chair/instructor. Let them make mistakes and learn from them. Since there is very little by way of research that the students can undertake to better understand their assigned country's preference, they normally align with their regional bid city. Again, if students do not fall in line with their region there is no need to instruct them otherwise.

At the conclusion of the second round of speeches, inform the delegates that the first vote will be taken. In accordance with the stated procedure, they may vote "Favorably" towards any or all of the host cities. Only positive votes by show of placard are counted. Using a blank version of the chart above, ask "All those in favor of Berlin indicate so by raising your placard." Count the votes and enter it into the Round 1 voting column for Berlin. Work your way through the other four bid cities and then announce which city has been eliminated by placing an X for it in columns two through five. When students return from the next caucus, and before speeches are made, announce the second round of voting. Note the totals and mark the second eliminated city. Allow speeches and then announce the next round of voting before a caucus session is allowed. Continue with this process until a city is selected to host the event.

Simulation Recap. By now, the students should be finding their footing and becoming more comfortable in simulation activities. They know to raise their placards during formal session to be recognized and they understand the most essential motion (move to caucus). This simulation takes their training to the next level by assigning to each student a country and putting them into a mildly competitive situation. This is the first simulation with a real-world feel and with delegates promoting a position based upon their country assignment. They will quickly research their country and determine which of the potential host countries is their closest ally.

In your recap, begin by reminding them that finding a solution to the challenge takes a back seat to securing their nation's interests. As such, they should have sought to "win" the bidding war by having their country's city selected. Inform the students that when they confront a simulation with minimal knowledge of their assigned country and the details of the challenge, reverting to regional alliances is the first step to take. Optimally, they should do a quick Google check to confirm that their assigned country has favorable relations with their region's bid-city country. I normally avoid this issue by not including among the placards countries that are hostle toward their neighbors and region.

Since many novice model diplomacy students do not have a background in the important role that regional groupings play in international organizations such as the United Nations, I provide the students with the regional groupings of UN members discussed the following week (4A). At some point during the conference, students will encounter a delegate representing a country that they are not familiar with. A quick check of the Regional Groupings document will give them an important data point.

Week 4A

Measuring Progress
Conference Flow
Working Groups

After the regional geography quiz, it is time to measure student progress in key areas. The first research binder check is a good place to start. Students should have completed their country background information collection. Roughly 25% of the binder is made up of information pertaining to the assigned country's government, economy, society, history and international relations. Ask students to locate in their binders various specific information, including the following:

Head of State/Government
Per Capital Income
Literacy Level
Country Map
Regional Map
World Map
UN Documents

It is perfectly fine not to have the information requested, but the students should note those areas of information that they may want to add to their binder. Emphasize that the research portfolio is their resource and that they should determine what information to include. The second binder check at week eight will include information about the committee and topics that they have been assigned.

The geography quiz and binder check were pre-announced, the next progress check is not. Below you will find the questions for an unannounced country knowledge quiz.

Official name of your country.
Continent(s) where you country is located.
Country size in square miles and/or in comparison to others.
Bordering state(s).
Regional bloc of your country.
Capital:
Currency:
Per capita income: $

Head of state:
Head of government:
Population size:
Type of government (democracy, monarchy, dictatorship, other).
Religious groups (largest to smallest).
Ethnic groups (largest to smallest).
Major rivers or lakes:.
Three largest cities by population.
Natural resources:
Primary export:
Primary import:
Closest ally:
Primary adversary:
Year your country joined the United Nations.

Short answer: In one or two sentences, explain how your country can justify taking a leading role in committee.

I give the students about fifteen minutes to work through the questions and then instruct them to put the document away and complete it at their leisure. I don't like to deflate their confidence by collecting and grading the pop quiz. The purpose is for them to realize the extent to which they are knowledgeable about their assigned country. The quiz also provides them with a study guide for the exam that takes place before the conference.

The Flow of a Diplomacy Conference

Week four is the optimal time to look forward to the conference and outline the basic flow of events once things get underway. Model diplomacy conferences may be rather brief, lasting only a day, or may take place over the course of a week. NMUN-DC begins on Friday afternoon with opening ceremony and concludes on Sunday evening with the awards ceremony. The New York version of NMUN is a Sunday through Thursday conference, with the bonus of using the United Nations headquarters for a session when the facility is available. Whether your delegation attends a brief or long conference, the process will be similar.

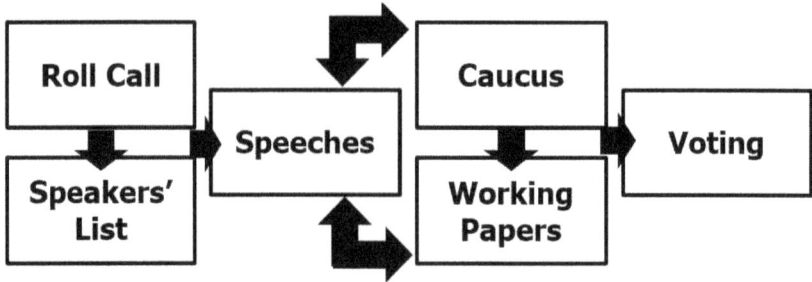

Once the formalities of starting the first committee session are complete, the process of moving towards resolution submission and voting takes on a predictable pattern. The speakers' list will open, allowing delegates to queue for agenda speeches. Being quick on the draw, especially when the speakers' list is populated using a portal, presents great opportunities to the well-prepared delegates. Some will have the chance to speak on both agenda setting and the first topic before others make a speech. Delivering two high-quality speeches right out of the gate signals to the committee (fellow delegates, the dais, judges) that you are a serious, engaged and well-prepared participant. Since speeches begin immediately, having formal speeches drafted before arriving at the conference is imperative. The committee will break into an informal caucus, allowing time for revisions that reflect developments with working groups. For multi-day conferences, caucus sessions will be forty-five minutes to an hour in length. During informal session, students move about the room in search of like-minded delegates.

Over the course of each session, the committee will toggle between formal and informal sessions. During formal sessions, speeches are delivered, motions are made, and documents are considered. Informal sessions are predominantly filled with small-group negotiations, speech writing and document preparation.

Working Groups

The most common organizing principle for caucus sessions is regional grouping, as introduced in the Week 3 simulation. International organizations typically use five geographic blocs (Africa, Asia, Latin America & the Caribbean, Eastern Europe and Western European & Others) as established by the United Nations at its founding. In the UN system, the blocs are used to balance representation on a variety of bodies and committees. In the Security Council, the ten two-year rotating (R10) seats are distributed across the five blocs. Judges to the International Court of Justice (ICJ) are elected by the Security Council and General Assembly with an eye towards regional representation by all blocs. The distribution of posts in many General Assembly committees relies upon regional blocs. Perhaps most importantly, regional groupings play a role in the selection of Secretaries General.

Established in 1945, the five regional blocs are less reflective of diplomatic patterns today because of the end of the Cold War. With the admission into the North Atlantic Treaty Organization (NATO) and the European Union (EU) of East European countries, the post-World War II geopolitical divide no longer exists. The East-West divide was not the only dynamic of the Cold War era, which also experienced the emergence of a Southern bloc (Africa, Asia, Latin America & the Caribbean) designed to counter the superpowers' dominance of the organization and promote an agenda that reflected Southern interests and concerns. The Southern bloc, also referred to as the Group of 77 (G77) or Non-Aligned Movement (NAM), remains a powerful force in universal committees with simple majority voting requirements. As indicated in the table below, the Southern bloc is made up of 140 United Nations member-states, which represents more than seventy percent of total members.

Number of United Nations Member-States in Each Regional Grouping/Bloc				
Africa	Asia	Eastern Europe	LA & Caribbean	WEOG
53	54	23	33	30

If the countries of Asia, Africa and Latin America & the Caribbean act in concert, they can pass any document in a committee with universal membership that adopts resolutions by a simple majority vote. There, however, are two problems with taking this approach. First, the member-states from the Non-Aligned Movement are diverse in terms of socio-economic development, form of government, priorities and interests. Reaching consensus among them is a difficult task. More importantly, for the document that they draft to have meaning and lead to action, they will need the support of the European countries. The membership in each of the five UN regional blocs is provided in the table below. Students are advised to include a copy of the table in their portfolios for reference during the conference.

United Nations Regional Blocs	
Africa	Algeria, Angola, Benin, Botswana, Burkina Faso, Burundi, Cabo Verde, Cameroon, Central African Republic, Chad, Comoros, Congo, Cote D'Ivoire, Democratic Republic of the Congo, Djibouti, Egypt, Equatorial Guinea, Eritrea, Eswatini, Ethiopia, Gabon, Gambia, Ghana, Guinea, Guinea-Bissau, Kenya, Lesotho, Liberia, Libya, Madagascar, Malawi, Mali, Mauritania, Mauritius, Morocco, Mozambique, Namibia, Niger, Nigeria, Rwanda, Sao Tome & Principe, Senegal, Seychelles, Sierra Leone, Somalia, South Africa, South Sudan, Sudan, Togo, Tunisia, Uganda, United Republic of Tanzania, Zambia, Zimbabwe
Asia	Afghanistan, Bahrain, Bangladesh, Bhutan, Brunei, Cambodia, China, Cyprus, Democratic People's Republic of (North) Korea, Fiji, India, Indonesia, Iran, Iraq, Japan, Jordan, Kazakhstan, Kiribati, Kuwait, Kyrgyzstan, Laos, Lebanon, Malaysia, Maldives, Marshall Islands, Micronesia, Mongolia, Myanmar, Nauru, Nepal, Oman, Pakistan, Palau, Papua New Guinea, Philippines, Qatar, Republic of (South) Korea, Samoa, Saudi Arabia, Singapore, Soloman Islands, Sri Lanka, Syria, Tajikistan, Thailand, Timor-Leste, Tonga, Türkiye, Turkmenistan, Tuvalu, United Arab Emirates, Uzbekistan, Vanuatu, Viet Nam, Yemen
Latin America & Caribbean	Antigua & Barbuda, Argentina, Bahamas, Barbados, Belize, Bolivia, Brazil, Chile, Colombia, Costa Rica, Cuba, Dominica, Dominican Republic, Ecuador, El Salvador, Grenada, Guatemala, Guyana, Haiti, Honduras, Jamaica, Mexico, Nicaragua, Panama, Paraguay, Peru, Saint Kitts & Nevis, Saint Lucia, Saint Vincent & Grenadines, Suriname, Trinidad & Tobago, Uruguay, Venezuela

Eastern Europe	Albania, Armenia, Azerbaijan Belarus, Bosnia, Bulgaria, Croatia, Czechia, Estonia, Georgia, Hungary, Kazakhstan, Kyrgyzstan, Latvia, Lithuania, Montenegro, Northern Macedonia, Republic of Moldova, Poland, Romania, Russia, Serbia, Slovakia, Slovenia, Tajikistan, Turkmenistan, Ukraine, Uzbekistan
Western Europe & Others	Andorra, Australia, Austria, Belgium, Canada, Denmark, Finland, France, Germany, Greece, Iceland, Ireland, Israel, Italy, Lichtenstein, Luxembourg, Malta, Monaco, Netherlands, New Zealand, Norway, Portugal, San Marino, Spain, Sweden, Switzerland, Türkiye, United Kingdom, United States

The problem with breaking into five regional groupings in large conferences is that there are still too many delegates in each bloc for the drafting of a single resolution. The proper strategy in model diplomacy is to identify three or four delegates who have a logical connection to work with. They may be from the same regional bloc but that is not mandatory. A delegate representing Madagascar could approach Cyprus and Jamaica and say "As fellow island nations, we should work together on a resolution. I have an idea, would you two like to work with Madagascar on a document?" Limiting yourself to a small caucus group creates several advantages for your student. Fewer voices translate to a higher common denominator for drafting a working paper. For most conferences, students working together use a shared document with editing/writing privileges extended to those in the inner circle (document sponsors). Having more than half-a-dozen document authors quickly becomes difficult to manage and to preserve the wedge issue that your student has placed at the center of the drafting effort. A small caucus group also makes your student, who invited the others to work together, the leader and unofficial spokesperson of the group. As the committee moves into the typical pattern of speakers, followed by caucus sessions, followed by speakers, the word of your student's working paper will get out. In fact, delegates want to announce that the "island" group is drafting a working paper. Others will ask to be added as sponsors (authors) of the working paper. This creates something of a dilemma for the small working group. Adding more sponsors builds out support that will be needed to submit the working paper as a resolution. Most conferences require 20% of the committee to support the document for it to move towards a formal vote. Adding sponsors, however, both dilutes the influence of your student and adds more people with editing rights. The solution to this problem is for the small group to agree to say to those who wish to join, "We appreciate your interest in our working paper. As we are far into the drafting process, we are not accepting any new sponsors, but we would love for you to become a signatory." A signatory is a country that expresses support for the document without becoming a sponsor. For the purposes of surpassing the 20% threshold established by the dais for a working paper to proceed to submission, both sponsors and signatories count towards the minimum number.

Week 4B

Simulation: Water Rights

A group of nations is meeting to discuss water rights in preparation for an upcoming international conference.

PARTIES: Nation-states represented by multiple delegates.

Draft, vote on and pass by simple majority as many resolutions as there are issues relating to the water rights topic. Resolutions are titled by the delegation that is submitting them. Each resolution must have at least one additional sponsor or signatory.

Schedule:

TIME (minutes)	ACTIVITY
	Roll Call
0-10	Caucus within Delegations
10-15	1-minute speeches
15-25	Open Caucus
25-30	1-minute speeches
30-35	Open Caucus
35-40	Vote on Resolutions

Prep Material. Country placards.

Directions for the Chair. Randomly assign countries to groups of three students. After roll call, follow the timeline outlined in the simulation. Remind the students that in the first caucus session, they are to speak only with delegates assigned to their country. When you return to formal session (minute 10), inform the first delegation/country that they have the floor for a period not to exceed 60 seconds. If they neglected to manage their time correctly, they would not have drafted a speech. Once all countries have made a speech, you may need to remind them that successful student delegates never deliver unprepared speeches. Your students should not make the mistake of attempting to make an impromptu speech for the remainder of the semester and it is wise for you to admonish them if they do.

Prior to the final caucus, inform the students that no documents need to be drafted as time is insufficient for a formal drafting process. Instead, delegations are to use their final speech to very briefly outline the water rights issue that they are proposing. As chair, announce the resolution number & sponsor (author) and ask for signatories.

For example:

Resolution 001   CANADA   Walter Filtration   Signatories are Laos & South Africa

After each water issue is announced by a delegation, ask delegations (not students) to vote YES, NO or ABSTAIN. If there are more YES votes than NO votes, indicate that the resolution has been adopted. Proceed until all issues are voted upon.

Simulation Recap. The simplicity of this simulation, with its highly choreographed structure and timeline, belies its importance and impact. It is here where students will learn about the single most important tool for their research, conference participation and ultimate success. What they learn from this recap will allow them to prepare to represent their assigned country impressively at the conference and succeed in passing resolutions. Understanding and identifying their individual "Wedge Issue" will also reduce prep time substantially. Use the remaining time in class to explain wedge issues, as outlined below.

Model diplomacy conferences are organized around a series of committees. In each committee, there will be at least one topic considered and as many as three. Student-delegates, therefore, must not only learn about their country and its relations with the world, but also about the topics assigned to their committee. The way to avoid overwhelming students is to require them to identify one aspect, or Wedge Issue, of the assigned topic that will be the focus of their research. Demonstrate how easy it is to find a wedge issue by brainstorming with the class on the water rights topic, listing as many different sub-topics within it. Diagram your ideas on the board. Next, narrow the focus of the wedge issue geographically. Students may seek to address the issue in one country that is in need, a sub-region, region or the world. Finally, determine exactly how the issue can be addressed by stating a solution.

TOPIC	SUB-TOPIC	RANGE	WEDGE ISSUE
Water Rights	Access	Sahara	Desalinization
Water Rights	Disease	Haiti	Cholera Kits
Water Rights	Dental Health	South America	Fluoridation
Water Rights	Packaging	G20 States	Plastic Reduction
Water Rights	Contamination	South Asia	Portable Purifiers

Instruct the students to identify one aspect of one of their assigned topics. For this example, let's assume that the student selects cholera test kits. That becomes the student's wedge issue, one portion (wedge) of the broader topic. After the student confirms that the wedge issue reflects her/his country's position, it becomes the focus of research until the conference. Each student-delegate should find a wedge issue for each topic assigned to their committee. If you are doubling up in a committee, both student-delegates will have their own distinct wedge issue for each topic. No longer must your students study all matters relating to the assigned topic (i.e., Water Rights), instead they will focus their research and write their speeches only about their wedge issue (Cholera Test Kits). This greatly reduces the amount of topic knowledge required and allows each student to specialize in one area of the broader topic. At the conference, they will join a small caucus group and suggest that its members work together to draft a resolution on the wedge issue.

Week 5A.

The Agenda Speech
Character of a Diplomat

After roll call and the regional geography quiz, attention turns to the first of three formal speeches that students will take to the conference: Agenda, Topic 1 and Topic 2. Diplomacy is, at its core, about dialogue. State representatives deliver formal speeches at their assigned diplomatic posts and to the general public. Being able to deliver prepared, relevant and properly presented speeches is key to success in model diplomacy. From my observations, roughly half of all speeches given at conferences are either unprepared, off-the-cuff presentations or lacking in at least one key aspect of successful speechmaking. In other words, if your students deliver proper formal speeches, beginning with the Agenda Speech, they will quickly place themselves in the top half of all participants. Delivering a successful speech sends all the right signals to three groups in the room. The first target audience is composed of the other student-delegates. Impressing them with a competent, properly delivered speech places your students in a favorable light. When the committee breaks into informal session, other delegates will naturally gravitate towards those who delivered impressive speeches. The second target audience is made up of members of the dais, which normally includes the committee chair, director and assistant director. These are the people who manage the sessions, entertain motions and monitor progress towards resolution consideration. You want your students to be viewed favorably by the dais, as often their decisions on whose raised placard to recognize or which resolutions should be merged greatly impact outcomes. The final target audience is made up of the judges. In most model diplomacies, awards are given to the most impressive delegates and delegations. A typical points scheme used by conferences is to award one point to the top 10% of delegates in each competitive session. A three-day conference will be organized around four to six sessions, separated by lunch and dinner breaks. If there are fifty countries in a committee, five delegates will receive a point in each session. The point totals are used at the conclusion of the conference to determine individual (delegate) and collective (delegation) awards. As noted earlier, only about one half of student-delegates deliver prepared speeches. Those who deliver thoroughly impressive, prepared speeches are a much smaller group. As I have instructed my students for decades, you cannot win points by delivering a proper diplomatic speech, but you can put yourself into the running by doing so. Add to a great speech active and constructive caucusing along with authoring a resolution and your chances of winning points increase greatly.

Model diplomacy conferences follow a basic flow from the adoption of the agenda to consideration of resolutions. Normally, the chair will gavel the session to order and spend some time explaining to delegates how the committee will address its agenda. An explanation of how the speakers' list works and links to voting procedure are commonplace. The first matter that must be addressed before any substantive action can be undertaken is the adoption of the agenda. Most conferences list two or three topics that the committee will consider, deliberate and attempt to resolve. While the agenda topics cannot be modified by the delegates, the order of the agenda must be set by them. If there are three topics, the options are 1-2-3, 1-3-2, 2-1-3, 2-3-1, 3-2-1, and 3-1-2. With three topics, agenda setting can take some time since there are so many options. Most major academic conferences assign only two topics per committee, greatly reducing the options to topic 1 followed by topic 2 or topic 2 followed by topic 1. The speakers' list will be opened, and delegates will indicate that they wish to be placed on the list either by raising their placard or using a portal set up by the conference. Since well-prepared students have drafted and practiced their agenda speech, they should ask to be placed on the speakers' list as soon as possible to increase the likelihood of being called forward to speak. Unlike with the longer consideration of topics, agenda debate happens quickly, and it is not uncommon for only a handful of delegates to be afforded the opportunity to speak. Once the speakers' list is populated and a limited number of speeches is delivered, a motion to suspend the meeting for the purposes of caucus is usually entertained and adopted. The committee breaks into informal session, where the delegates move about the room and discuss the preferred order of topic consideration. When the caucus time expires, the committee automatically moves into formal session with student-delegates seated, quiet and attentive. Formal speeches resume until a delegate stands to motion for the adoption of the agenda "…as follows, topic 1 followed by topic 2." The motion requires a second, this indicates that at least one other delegate supports the motion, and then a simple-majority vote is taken. On procedural matters, delegates may vote YES or NO, ABSTAIN is not an option. Voting may be by show of placards or conducted electronically. If the motion receives the support of a majority of votes, the agenda is set. If not, a motion to adopt the agenda with another order option is made. This continues until the agenda is set. It is important to note that non-votes are not counted, only YES and NO votes are tabulated. When the agenda is adopted, the speakers' list is wiped clean, and the committee begins consideration of the topic selected by the committee. A new speakers' list is opened, and student-delegates populate it.

There are many ways to draft an agenda speech. The delegate may focus exclusively on the preferred order of topics or instead endorse both topics as worthy of consideration without stating an order preference. The speech can be about the assigned country's past efforts to resolve one or more of the topics. It can explain the issue's impact from a local, regional or global perspective. In other words, there is no "right" way to draft an agenda speech, only a correct way to deliver it. Use the rubric provided in Week 2a to score each of your students as they deliver their agenda speeches.

Diplomatic & Country Character

Central to model diplomacy competence is an understanding of character, both country and diplomatic. Remaining in country character means that the student-delegates accurately reflect the interests and policies of their assigned country. When delegates from the Democratic People's Republic of Korea and the Republic of Korea work closely together, it is almost always a violation of country character. The same can be said of Israel and Iran or the United States and Cuba. While conference organizers aim for an accurate representation of world affairs in their simulations, they do not want to squelch the creativity and novel ideas of the students who participate. Otherwise, simulations would be overly scripted and restrictive. To encourage student imagination and to unearth new ways of addressing old problems, model diplomacy conferences allow "creative diplomacy" that may veer slightly from real world politics. Students, however, should not view this as a carte blanche authority to disregard their assigned country's stated positions. Minor, and at times major, violations of country character happen at every model diplomacy conference and all but the most egregious are usually overlooked by organizers and judges. We all understand that these are students and not professional diplomats, some divergence from official state policy is expected and excused.

Diplomatic character is another matter, with little allowances for violations. Diplomats act and interact in highly professional, disciplined and controlled ways. In the conduct of their formal affairs, they are serious and direct. From my experience, diplomatic character must be taught and reinforced throughout the training protocol. If you allow students to joke around, laugh during deliberations, arrive late and act unprofessionally in class, they will carry those bad habits forward and will not be viewed positively by their fellow delegates, members of the dais and judges at the conference. I begin gently in weeks two and three by reminding students that they need to tighten up their behavior and by week four I admonish them for their violations. Students who arrive late at class due to parking lot issues or personal emergencies also arrive late at formal sessions at the conference for completely different reasons. Punctuality is a habit that must be formed. In my class, students lose points if they are not in their seats at the start of class or if they neglected to bring their placards to class. Students rise to expectations. When it comes to diplomatic character instructors need to set the bar very high and consistently reinforce it. Only serious delegations can be highly competitive and well considered by others.

Week 5B.

Simulation: Self-Determination

After Kosovo declared its independence from Serbia, several entities made similar proclamations of independence (see list below):

DECLARATION OF INDEPENDENCE	CURRENT STATE
Scotland	United Kingdom
Flanders	Belgium
Basque	France
Catalonia	Spain
South Ossetia	Georgia
Palestine	Israel

A meeting of interested parties has been convened to discuss the string of declarations of independence. Each participant is entitled to vote YES, NO, ABSTAIN on each resolution. The participants agreed to consider a limited range of outcomes, as listed below:

1. Recognition of any or all independence bids and full United Nations membership.

   This option requires a super-majority of votes (2/3), including the concurring votes of the permanent members of the UN Security Council (China, France, Russia, United Kingdom, United States).

2. Recognition of one or more of the independence bids.

   This option requires a super-majority of votes (2/3).

3. Joint statement supporting a negotiated settlement of the independence bids.

   This option requires a simple majority of votes.

4. Rejection of any or all the independence bids.
   This option requires a simple majority of votes.

The nations (Russia, India, Sri Lanka, Nigeria) that opposed the independence bid of Kosovo had warned that its recognition would trigger additional independence claims.

The nations (US, France, Australia, UK, Germany) that supported Kosovo's independence now must determine how to prevent these new bids from succeeding without appearing hypocritical.

Other nations (Cuba, North Korea, Iran) view independence bids of all people with favor as a matter of principle and as a means of distracting the attention of the major powers and undermine their unity.

Resolutions must indicate which category (1-4) is applicable.

Time Limit: 60 minutes.

Prep Material. Provide as many country placards as you have students, beginning with the aspirant new countries and their current states.

Directions for the Chair. This is the most complicated simulation to date, but by week five your students should be up to the challenge. For the first time, they are required to draft a document for each proposed resolution, although you should not require a great deal of sophistication or detail. Resolution writing comes later in the training protocol. The students should be adept at making motions to caucus, multitasking during the informal sessions and delivering prepared speeches. Since the voting threshold changes depending on option selected, it is important to properly assign the category (1-4) of each drafted resolution.

Simulation Recap. Placing students in assigned roles reinforces the need of delegates to act in ways that reflect the interests of their country. A lesson that should be learned in this simulation is that compromise is often required to reach a sufficient consensus to adopt a resolution. Often, student-delegates begin with significant demands, such as the independence of one or more aspirant independent states (options 1 & 2). Because the voting bar is set high for these two options, they quickly learn that they need to revise their demands to qualify for a lower voting threshold (options 3 & 4).

Week 6A

Topic Speech
Wedge Issue Review
Rules of Order

After roll call it is time for the first topic speech. Use the rubric provided in week 2A and notify students of deficiencies. The wedge issue was introduced to students in week 4A, it is important to return to the subject to see how students are progressing in terms of finding their narrow aspect of the assigned topic to focus their research on. The most common problem with wedge issue development is vagueness. For example, on the United Nations Environment Assembly (UNEA) one of the two topics is Addressing Marine Plastic Pollution. It is not enough for a student to say that their wedge issue is reducing plastic waste, they must be much more specific. A successful wedge issue will have three components: target, challenge and policy. The **target** may be geographic or refer to the group or activity whose actions will be changed by the wedge issue. **Challenge** means the specific issue being addressed, what will be fixed by the wedge issue, and **Policy** relates to the action that will be taken. Additionally, each wedge issue should have a name, or handle, that others will remember and associate with the issue.

Target	Challenge	Policy	Name
Cruise Ships	Plastic Straws	On Demand	Straws Blow
Fishing Industry	Plastic Parts	Alternative Parts	Safe Fishing

The two examples above meet all four requirements. In the first, the resolution will call upon cruise ships to voluntarily provide straws in drinks upon request, rather than automatically including one in each drink. This would dramatically cut down on the number of plastic straws used, disposed of and ending up in the ocean or waterway. In the second, the resolution will educate the fishing industry of the high level of plastic parts found in fishing gear (65%) and suggest marine-safe alternatives. Few students in week six will have fully developed wedge issues. This is a good time to brainstorm with the class in search of issues that meet the above criteria.

Rules of Order

Rules of procedure are used by groups to create order in deliberative settings. In model diplomacy conferences, they allow delegates to complete their assigned tasks in a methodical fashion without advantaging large groups of participants over smaller ones. Technically, the role of a committee chair is limited to serving as the administrator of delegate motions. Chairs can be highly influential in preventing the abuse of rules and maintaining a flow of activities that allows delegates to complete their assigned tasks in a timely manner. Strong chairs will encourage motions at the appropriate time and determine unnecessary motions to be dilatory and, thus, not subject to consideration. All chairs should explain the implications of motions as well as the requirements for consideration of them.

The rules of order are divided into four categories: main motions, subsidiary motions, incidental motions, and renewal motions. Some motions take precedent over others, such that it is not the order in which the motions are made that determine their order of consideration. Some motions are required to be dealt with before less important, or subservient, ones. For those wishing to become highly knowledgeable about rules of procedure, I suggest a copy of *Robert's Rules of Parliamentary Order*. It would be a mistake, in my opinion, to spend a great deal of time learning and practicing the rules, as doing so comes at the expense of proper and thorough investigation of country backgrounds, topics and skills training.

The table below outlines the most common motions that a student-delegate will encounter and should be prepared to use and respond to in a typical academic model diplomacy conference. Others will be raised rarely and should be explained fully by the chair prior to consideration and vote.

Most Common Rules of Order		
MOTION	**PURPOSE**	**VOTE**
Adoption of the Agenda	Set the order of the topics	Majority
Change Speaking Time	Increases or decreases time	2 speak for, 2 speak against. Majority
Point of Order	Correct a mistake by the chair	Chair rules on the motion
Suspension of the Meeting	Move to informal caucus	Majority
Adjourn Debate	Immediately end consideration of topic	2 speak for, 2 speak against. Majority
Closure of Debate	Move into formal voting	2 speak against. 2/3 majority

Points of order are pretty rare and closure of debate is equally infrequent, but may be raised by delegates either attempting to play an outsized role in proceedings or to avoid running out of time. Suspension of the meeting is, by far, the most used motion since it allows participants to move into informal session to caucus with other delegates and draft documents. The adjournment of debate occurs when there are speakers on the list but there is a consensus that further discussion is unnecessary to complete the committee's tasks. Because the motion infringes on the right of those delegates on the speakers' list from addressing the body, it allows four delegates to make brief statements in favor or against the motion. This presents a golden opportunity for well-prepared delegates to shine where most others come up short. Few delegates prepare a 10-second for/against speech, doing so indicates to the dais and judges that you are truly prepared for the simulation. Below are several for/against statements that a delegate can rise to state at the appropriate time. While the motion to close debate in order to move directly into formal voting is the most common, I have included similar statements for other motions that require brief speeches. Students making these short speeches do not normally go to the podium, rather they stand at their seats and speak to the committee. As you will see, country name is included in each speech for the same reasons that it is used repeatedly in formal speeches. Students can practice these statements a few times in class in preparation for the conference, if for no other reason than to polish their public speaking skills.

Motion to Close Debate/ Call the Question

Against the Motion: Fellow delegates, CANADA strongly opposes the motion to close debate. Work remains to be done on the resolutions that have been drafted, moving directly to voting at this time prevents delegates on the speakers' list from expressing their views on this topic. As such, CANADA stands in opposition to this motion and encourages other delegates to do so as well.

Motion to Adjourn Debate

In Favor of the Motion: Fellow delegates, CANADA wishes to state its reluctant support of the motion to adjourn consideration of this topic. After countless hours of speeches, debate and resolution writing, it is evident that this body cannot attain sufficient consensus to advance to voting on resolutions. As such, CANÀDA supports this motion and encourages other delegates to do so as well so that we can move on to the next topic on the agenda.

Against the Motion: Fellow delegates, CANADA strongly opposes the motion to adjourn debate. Progress made to this point is worthy of continuation of our collective efforts. As such, CANADA stands in opposition to this motion and encourages other delegates to oppose it as well.

Motion to Increase Speaking Time

In Favor of the Motion: Fellow delegates, it is imperative that members of this body be allowed to properly and fully address the issue before us. As such, CANADA supports this motion and encourages other delegates to do so as well.

Against the Motion: Fellow delegates, it is imperative that all members of this body wishing to formally voice their positions on this important issue be afforded the privilege to do so. Increasing the speaking time will limit the number of speakers allowed to address this committee. As such, CANADA opposes this motion and encourages other delegates to oppose it as well.

Motion to Decrease Speaking Time

In Favor of the Motion: Fellow delegates, it is imperative that members of this body be able to address the issue before us. Limiting the speaking time allows more voices to be heard on this important issue. As such, CANADA supports the motion and encourages other delegates to support it as well.

Against the Motion: Fellow delegates, the complexities of this topic require sufficient time for those wishing to speak to adequately express their positions. As such, CANADA opposes this motion and encourages other delegates to do so as well.

Week 6B

Simulation: Trust or Betrayal

Three countries make claims to Kashmir, a region at the core of multiple wars since the United Kingdom decolonized its South Asia territorial possessions after World War II. The three parties to the dispute (India, Pakistan, China) historically controlled their unofficial 'zones' of Kashmir with armed forces on the periphery. Tensions commonly run high as each state fears that one of the others will launch a full-scale invasion and effectively control the territory. Thus, invasion by one or more parties is a constant threat to peace and security.

Scenarios and Payoffs

SCENARIO 1. All three parties elect to invade.

  PAYOFF: A trilateral war with no side able to overcome the others results in a stalemate. All sides receive 10 out of 20 points.

SCENARIO 2. Two of the three states elect to invade.

  PAYOFF: The two invading countries halve the region. Each invading state receives 15 points. The country that opted to stay out loses all control and scores zero points out of 20.

SCENARIO 3. One of the three states elects to invade.

  PAYOFF: The invading country seizes control of Kashmir. The invading country receives 18 points. The two countries that did not invade lose control over the region. They each receive five points out of 20.

SCENARIO 4: All three parties elect to not invade.

  PAYOFF: All three countries receive full credit (20 points) for the simulation.

Two delegates will be assigned as the United States and the UK, their assignment is to promote scenario 4. Delegates representing the USA and UK will receive the average number of points as the delegates assigned to China, India and Pakistan.

Time Limit: 60 minutes

Prep Material. Placards for India, Pakistan, China, USA, UK.

Directions for the Chair. This is a classic three-way Prisoners' Dilemma where cooperation to avoid war is often undermined by distrust. Divide all but two of your participants into three country groups (India, Pakistan, China) and assign one student each to represent the United States and United Kingdom. Provide the five country placards and allow the simulation to unfold as normal. Wait until it is time for the final decision (Invade, Do Not Invade) before announcing that voting will happen in isolation. Make sure that the delegations are separated from each other to limit espionage and signaling of intention.

Provide each of three states (India, China, Pakistan) directly involved in the territorial dispute with a ballot and ask them to indicate their final decision. No communication is allowed between the parties, and the two observers (United States and United Kingdom) have no further role to play even though their fate is tied to the outcome. Give the delegations three minutes and then require them to make their choice and fold the paper in half. Collect the three voting ballots but do not look at the responses and announce the outcome until after the recap.

Simulation Recap. Briefly explain the Prisoners' Dilemma (PD) game theory using the chart provided below to demonstrate that in similar circumstances rational actors will choose a sub-optimal outcome (Quadrant IV) to avoid the worse-case scenario (Quadrants II or III).

Prisoners' Dilemma begins with the detention of two individuals suspected of stealing diamonds. The police have no hard evidence and hope to "flip" one or both defendants by enticing them to confess their crime in exchange for a reduced sentence. The suspects are placed in separate rooms and offered a deal: confess your crime before the other one does. If both prisoners remain loyal to each other, the police will not have enough evidence to convict and they both go free. If one confesses and provides incriminating evidence on the other, he or she receives a lesser sentence. If both confess, they receive a jail sentence in between the two extremes. The table below illustrates the Payoffs for the four Quadrants for each suspect.

		Prisoner 1	
		Remain Loyal	Confess
Prisoner 2	Remain Loyal	I Both Set Free	II Prisoner 1: 1 Year Prisoner 2: 10 Years
	Confess	III Prisoner 1: 10 Years Prisoner 2: 1 Year	IV Both Serve 3 Years

If some or all your students elect to invade Kashmir, it is important to inform them that they have not failed the simulation since in prisoners' dilemma the most common outcome is failure (Quadrant IV). Rational actors will avoid the risk of taking the full blame/punishment and therefore defect (confess).

Instructors should then explain that the way to escape the fate of the Prisoners' Dilemma is to rearrange the "game" away from zero-sum and towards mutually beneficial. Stag Hunt is such a game. Four hunters work together to trap and kill a deer, planning to share the plentiful bounty if successful. Each is positioned in such a way that they drive the stag towards a cliff. While waiting, one of the hunters spots a rabbit and must decide whether to remain loyal to the group in its quest for the stag or satisfy his immediate interests by leaving his post and chasing the rabbit. His default response is to remain loyal to the group since defecting will result in him no longer being invited to group hunts in the future.

If you opt not to introduce the intricacies of game theory, simply tell your students that the lesson to be learned is that if you cannot trust members of your own delegation during a practice session, you cannot count of the support of students from other schools at the conference. Delegates commonly promise to support resolutions that they end up voting against.

Week 7A

Position Paper Rough Drafts
Binder Check
Resolution Writing

With the deadline approaching for the submission of position papers to the conference, week seven is the time to conduct a first review of the documents. Position papers are submitted by delegations, not by individual delegates. In other words, if you have a delegation of fourteen students who represent a country on seven committees, your school is responsible for submitting seven position papers. It is the number of committees, not the number of student-delegates, that determines how many position papers are required.

Committee partners collaborate on the drafting of the position paper and bring a print copy to class for the first review. Collect and redistribute the position papers, making sure that no one is reviewing their own document. If you assign two students per committee, do the same for the review process. Projecting a sample position paper on the screen and walking the class through the format requirements while asking them to mark discrepancies is a good way to start. Verify line spacing, font size, margins and other paper requirements (bold, italic, centered, etc.) before actually reading the text of the documents.

Then ask the students to read through the papers and mark any areas that may need additional attention. If in-class review of draft position papers is the only check of the documents before final drafts are due, plan for this process to take 45 minutes to an hour. It is a tedious process but vital to the submission of proper position papers. Some schools rely upon experienced model diplomacy students to further review position papers for both format compliance and paper quality. Some programs create a "bank" of position papers drafted over the years for future delegates to review and consider as templates for their document. In my opinion, it is in the best interests of students to draft their position papers from scratch. Going through the process is an important step in conference preparation. Unfortunately, the temptation to rely upon modern technologies and software systems lures many students to shortcut the drafting process for the purpose of completing the assignment with as little time and effort possible. The use of artificial intelligence (AI) is rapidly becoming commonplace in all facets of life, personal and professional. Academia is no exception. Most conferences prohibit the use of AI for the drafting of speeches, position papers and conference resolutions. It is a challenge, to say the least, for instructors and team leaders to monitor the use of AI by students. At a minimum, we should inform the students that the use of AI is not only prohibited but also undermines their development as young professionals. Reinforcing the importance of crafting model diplomacy documents without the assistance of AI should be done at various points in the training protocol.

Binder Check

Week seven is also a research binder check, the second of the semester. By this point, the binders should be sixty percent filled and some organization of materials evident. For the second portfolio check, ask the students for the following information:

Topic Background Guide
UN Resolutions on the Topic
Speeches Made by the Assigned Country on Topic
UN Organizational Chart
Agenda Speech
Topic 1 Speech
Regional Blocs

Every international organization (United Nations, NATO, EU, OAS, Arab League) has a founding document, usually an international treaty, that defines its powers and responsibilities. Having a copy of the organization's founding document in the binder is the norm, but few students will possess a working knowledge of its many provisions. For the United Nations, there are several sections, articles or chapters, that should be at the delegate's fingertips. These concepts and provisions can be included in speeches, discussed during informal session negotiations and referenced in resolutions. The chart below lists the articles and chapters often referenced in resolutions. For conferences that simulate other international organizations, a similar table should be constructed for students for inclusion in their research binders.

Key United Nations Charter Provisions	
Preamble	Reaffirms faith in human rights, including the equal rights of men and women and of nations large and small.
Article 2(4)	Prohibition on the use, or threat of the use of force, in international relations.
Article 33	Mandates the peaceful settlement of disputes.
Article 51	The right of self-defense and collective self-defense in response to an armed attack until such time that the Security Council can respond.
Article 94(2)	States that the Security Council can enforce the decisions of the International Court of Justice (ICJ).
Article 99	Empowers the UN Secretary General to call the Security Council into session.
Chapter 6&1/2	Informal name given to a peacekeeping operation (PKO) that arrives after a conflict has concluded and with the consent of parties to the dispute. Also known as "traditional" or "first generation" peacekeeping.
Chapter 6&3/4	Informal name given to a peacekeeping operation (PKO) that enters an ongoing conflict. Also known as "non-traditional" or "second generation" peacekeeping.
Chapter 7	Grants the Security Council power to authorize the use of armed force in response to a threat to international peace and security.

Even though your group is slightly more than half-way through the training protocol, they should be 75-80% ready for the conference. Their speaking skills are increasingly sharpened, research binders approaching presentable condition and they have completed enough simulations to have a feel for the flow of the conference. Most of their time in committee will be spent with the group of student-delegates who they are working with on a resolution.

Over the course of the simulation, the chair will indicate that it is time to start submitting working papers for consideration and a deadline a short time later will be announced. This is when the sponsors, authors of the document, want to shift into promotion gear by spreading out through the room and informing other delegates about the substance of the working paper, answering questions raised and eliciting signatory commitments. This is not the time to offer major changes to the document since that may jeopardize timely submission and cause other signatories to drop out if they don't approve the changes.

Submission of the working paper to the chair is normally done electronically. Some conferences do little to the documents other than assign to them a number (e.g., Resolution 001) and distribute them to the committee for review. At major academic conferences with significant volunteer support staff, the documents are scrutinized for formatting or spelling errors and returned to the sponsors for revision before being accepted as a draft resolution. Staff will also consider the working papers in relation to others, looking for those that are similar in content.

Once identified, the chair will direct the sponsors of the two (or more) resolutions to merge them. This is a very difficult task as the number of sponsors may be high, time is short, compromise is required, and energy levels are low. It is the sort of thing that your students must simply muscle through if they want their resolution to be considered for adoption. What your students should never do is resist the instructions of the chair to merge documents. The chair and his/her staff have already made this determination before informing the sponsors of the working papers and isn't often in the mood for an argument about the decision. Your students will gain additional respect from the chair if they respond "Yes, Honorable Chair, we will get right to it."

When the working papers have been accepted, labeled as resolutions and assigned a number, the committee is ready for final discussion and formal voting procedure. Amendments, or changes to the document, can be offered. The chair should walk the committee through the process of considering amendments. The resolution is then voted upon by the committee. In most instances, each delegate will have one vote and a simple majority of those voting YES or NO determines the outcome. While on procedural matters, such as voting on motions to caucus, delegates have only the option of voting YES or NO, on substantive matters such as resolutions a third option is available, the abstention. To ABSTAIN is to vote neither in favor or against a resolution. The only time that a delegate does not have the option of abstaining on a resolution is if they announced during roll call of the current session "Present and Voting." If they, instead, responded with "Present" during roll call they have all three voting options.

There are times when a show of placards for a simple majority vote is not taken. It is not unusual at the beginning of voting on a resolution for a delegate to move for "Adoption by Acclamation." If there are no objections, the document is adopted without a formal vote. This not only saves time for the committee, but also allows dissenters to avoid publicly voting against a resolution. Taking more time than either a show of placards or adoption by acclamation is the dreaded roll call vote. Any member of the committee may move for a roll call vote. The committee is duty bound by the rules of order to conduct voting on a delegate-by-delegate basis. Neither chairs nor fellow delegates warmly receive a roll call vote, so it is not often the best strategy and is prohibited by some academic conferences. The only time that a motion to hold a roll call vote is useful is if there is the desire to force delegates to individually reveal their vote on the resolution.

Resolution Writing

Before votes on a document can be taken, however, the resolution must be drafted. The aim of a model diplomacy committee is to adopt documents that resolve the assigned topic, in whole or in part. Students should remember that most of the issues addressed by the United Nations are not new to the organization's agenda, rather they are persistent problems in world affairs that have been addressed over a long period of time. As such, the aim of a model diplomacy student is not to wholistically "solve" the challenge but to move the needle in that direction on a narrow slice of the issue. Each student should work with their small caucus group to draft a document that focuses on their wedge issue. If two students are teamed together, representing the same country on a committee, it is optimal for them to each assemble a small caucus group and draft separate resolutions. This gives the delegation a two-for-one impact on deliberations, one country drafting two separate and distinct resolutions. This can only happen, of course, if both students assigned to the committee have their own wedge issue for the topic under consideration.

Most conferences, and all the more established ones, provide an electronic resolution template that student-delegates use to draft their documents. Students in the small caucus group, each with editing privileges, is considered a sponsor, or author, of the document they are collectively working on. Over the course of the conference, the document will be developed as students draft preambular clauses and operative clauses. The table below lists the commonly used clauses in UN resolutions with an explanation of each category.

Preambular Clauses.

Affirming	Alarmed by	Approving	Bearing in mind
Believing	Confident	Contemplating	Convinced
Declaring	Deeply concerned	Deeply conscious	Deeply disturbed
Deeply regretting	Desiring	Emphasizing	Expecting
Fulfilling	Fully alarmed	Fully aware	Fully believing
Further deploring	Further recalling	Guided by	Having adopted
Having considered	Having examined	Having heard	Having received
Having studied	Keeping in mind	Noting with regret	Noting with concern
Noting further	Observing	Reaffirming	Realizing
Recalling	Recognizing	Referring	Seeking
Taking into account	Taking note	Welcoming	

The preambular clauses state the issues that the drafting group seeks to address on the issue. They can be used to explain the reasons behind the group's work and highlight past international attention and efforts on the issue. It is common to use preambular clauses that reference specific United Nations resolutions, international treaties and provide background information on the topic. Preambular clauses set the table for action that is called for in the second portion of the resolution.

Operative Clauses.

Accepts	Affirms	Approves	Authorizes
Calls	Condemns	Confirms	Condemns
Confirms	Congratulates	Considers	Declares accordingly
Deplores	Designates	Draws the attention	Emphasizes
Encourages	Endorses	Expresses its hope	Further invites
Further acclaims	Further reminds	Further recommends	Further requests
Further resolves	Has resolved	Notes	Proclaims
Reaffirms	Recommends	Regrets	Reminds
Requests	Solemnly affirms	Strongly condemns	Supports
Takes note of	Transmits	Trusts	

Operative clauses outline the solution being proposed to address the challenge. It is important that the operative clauses are specifically linked to the issues raised in the preambular clauses in the first half of the resolution. While not required, the document should be relatively balanced with roughly the same number of preambular and operative clauses.

As the drafting process evolves over the course of several informal caucus sessions, a key aim of the drafters of the document is to inform the committee of the work that the group is conducting. This can be done in two ways, through inter-group caucus notification and by making speeches in formal session. As other delegates learn of the work of the small group, the sponsors will be notified of their interest in being designated a signatory of the resolution. Signatories do not have editing privileges and do not make alterations of the document as it is being drafted. They may suggest or request revisions, but the final arbiter of edits is the drafting group of sponsors. When a delegate declares an interest in being designated as a signatory, he or she is officially stating support for the document. As noted earlier, most conferences have a minimum threshold of sponsors and signatories, requiring, for example, that 20% of delegations in the committee must be stated as one or the other before the document can be submitted to the dais.

Getting to 50%+1.

As the working paper develops over the course of several informal caucus sessions, attention must be paid to garnering sufficient votes to adoption. For the most part, model diplomacy conference committees require a simple majority of YES votes. For the Security Council, the voting rules are different. In the Council, a resolution must obtain nine YES votes and avoid a NO vote from a permanent member (P5). With fifteen delegations, the Council threshold is three-fifths of full membership. Absences and abstentions do not affect the minimum nine-vote threshold. For most committees, however, a simple majority is required for passage. There, as well, abstentions are not factored into the YES-NO calculation. In a committee with eighty delegations, a total of forty-one YES votes guarantees that the document will be adopted. If the small caucus group has five sponsors and sixteen signatories, it is more than halfway to passage. The surest way to lock down additional votes for the document is to add more signatories. It should be noted, however, that there is neither a guarantee nor requirement for signatories to vote in favor of the resolution. If the document changes, either during further deliberations or via an amendment during formal voting session, the signatory may have second thoughts. In addition to building up the number of potential YES votes, the sponsors of the resolution can increase the chance of passage by encouraging non-supporting delegates to ABSTAIN on the resolution. As noted earlier, abstentions only lower the number of votes taken and are not considered for passage. The table below illustrates the fluidity in the vote requirements for a resolution.

Outcomes With Votes With Eighty Countries in a 50%+1 Committee.

Resolution	YES	NO	ABSTAIN	RESULT
1	80	0	0	Adopted
2	39	39	2	Not Adopted
3	34	32	14	Adopted

It should be noted that while resolution 2 received more votes in favor (39) than resolution 3 (34), it was not adopted. The larger number of abstentions in the vote on resolution 3 resulted in a simple majority of YES/NO votes and, thus, adoption. Converting potential NO votes to ABSTAIN often requires changing the resolution. Delegates should weigh the value of increased votes against the impact of revising the document to increase support, or conversely to lower opposition. Sometimes it is better to narrowly pass a resolution that fully reflects the interests of the sponsors, at other times it is better to gain widespread support for a document that mostly resolves the issue or reflects the interests of the sponsors. That is a judgement call that student-delegates must make on the floor during the conference.

Voting.

According to *Robert's Rules of Order*, voting on documents can take place under two circumstances—when the speakers' list is exhausted or when the committee successfully moves via motion into voting. It is rare for the speakers' list to be exhausted, in fact, most of the time the speakers' list needs to be closed so that the committee can more easily move into voting procedure when the documents are ready for consideration. Chairs will guide the committee in such a way that the many documents being drafted are ready for consideration at the same time and before the conference closes. This is not an issue at the United Nations since the organization operates year-round. If a resolution is not ready for consideration by the committee when the current session closes, the issue is placed on the agenda of the next session. At model diplomacy conferences, however, there is a firm end date and time established by the conference organizers. It is imperative, therefore, that all work on documents be completed with ample time for the committee to undertake voting procedures.

When the committee is moved into formal voting, each resolution is considered in the order determined by the dais. In large conferences involving thousands of students, it is not unusual for more than a dozen resolutions to be queued up for consideration in each committee. While a specified list of sponsors and signatories are listed for working documents, once the resolutions are approved by the dais for consideration the names are removed as the document is the property of the committee.

The first step is the amendment process. At some conferences, amending a resolution is as simple as making a motion to amend. The change in the resolution is stated and the delegates vote in favor or against the amendment. At larger conferences, where amending resolutions can delay voting substantially, delegates are required to submit formal documents in advance for approval by the dais.

If the amendment is approved, the resolution is changed to reflect the alteration. If the motion to amend is not approved, the resolution is not changed. There is no limit on the number of amendments that can be proposed. The only restriction on amending resolutions is the prohibition of "violating the spirit of the document." For example, a motion to amend the resolution by raising desired contributions to a project from 2% to 3% is allowable. Moving to change the phrase "Supports the independence movement..." to "Rejects the independence movement..." is not allowed as it clearly violates the spirit of the document.

When there are no additional amendment requests, the resolution is put to formal vote. Delegates may vote YES, NO or ABSTAIN. Before the era of the Internet and web-based hubs, the raising of placards for each vote was the only option. In large conferences, this could add hours to voting since accurately counting hundreds of placards for yes, no and abstain is challenging. For the most part today, conferences allow voting on cell phones through an established webpage or hub. As such, even large committees can move through voting procedure on a dozen resolutions very quickly. After votes are tabulated on a resolution, the results are announced (adopted or not adopted).

Once all resolutions are fully considered and voted upon, the committee moves on to the next topic assigned to the committee. The speakers' list is wiped clean, and a new one is opened. This is not the time for your student, fresh off the elation of drafting a resolution that was adopted, to relax and let others take the lead. She/he has prepared for the next topic, has a wedge issue and should follow the same assertive, yet collaborative, strategy used for the previous topic.

Week 7B

Simulation: Crisis in Africa

South Sudan gained its independence in 2011, breaking away from the Republic of Sudan through a complex negotiated process. Tensions between the two countries have been high, resulting in armed conflict. It was reported by the BBC yesterday that troops from Sudan had entered South Sudan and had taken control of an oil field. South Sudan has asked the international community to impose sanctions on Sudan and to provide military assistance to oust the foreign troops.

Three delegations (Sudan, South Sudan, European Union) will debate the issue and seek to resolve it. All participating delegates must make at least one thirty-second speech and at least one resolution must be submitted for a vote.

Time Limit: 60 minutes.

Prep Material.   Placards for Sudan, South Sudan, European Union.

Instructions.   By this time, students should seamlessly move between formal and informal sessions, making speeches and outlining possible resolution ideas as the simulation unfolds.

Recap. This simulation provides a great opportunity for student-delegates to reference important Charter provisions outlined in Week 7A. The principle of 'sovereign integrity' is central to the world politics and the global legal order. The United Nations Charter (1945) is the legal treaty that founded the organization. Its Article 2(4) protects the sovereignty, territorial integrity and political independence of all member states. Respect for sovereignty is not only legally mandated but is a source of stability in international relations. Article 33 mandates the peaceful settlements of disputes and Chapters VI and VII refer to peacekeeping operations and enforcement actions, respectively.

In this simulation, students should not quickly dismiss the sovereign claims of South Sudan or overlook the importance of Sudan's violation of the integrity of its southern neighbor. Diplomacy isn't just about reaching an agreement that ends an ongoing conflict, although that is certainly an important aim. Additionally, negotiated settlements must consider violators of the rules that govern states and hold them accountable. Article 33 calls upon member-states to resolve their disputes by peaceful means. A resolution could call for the UN Secretary General to invoke his powers under Article 99 to call the Security Council into session to address the issue. Using relevant Charter articles in resolutions is an excellent way to strengthen the document and garner support from others.

Week 8A

Topic 2 Line Speeches
The "Hot Seat"

Students have delivered two formal speeches in class to date, the Agenda and Topic 1 speeches. In week eight, they deliver their second topic speech. While it is perfectly fine to call students to the podium individually to deliver their speech, I like to mix things up with "Line Speeches." As its name suggests, students in groups of three come to the front of the class and stand side by side to simultaneously deliver their speeches. If they represent the same country, they will speak in unison at first.

Honorable Chair, Fellow Delegates. The Sultanate of Oman...

From there, the speeches diverge. While you will not be able to clearly hear each student's speech, this exercise trains them to deliver speeches under less-than-ideal conditions. Speaking in class is significantly less challenging than doing so in front of a large audience using a microphone, with the normal background noise associated with a conference. Concentrating on delivering their speeches despite having a fellow delegate beside them doing the same is great practice for the imperfect conditions associated with large settings. An additional benefit of Line Speeches is that it takes one-third the time of individual speeches, leaving more time for week eight's Hot Seat exercise.

The Hot Seat

At this point in the preparation schedule, students will have a firm grasp of their country's interests and policies, particularly as they relate to the topics assigned to their respective committees. They have selected a wedge issue for each of their topics but are untested in the actual "pitch" that they will give to promote it. The Hot Seat exercise gives them that opportunity and takes them one step closer to being conference ready. It is important that each student has her or his own wedge issue for each topic. If you've assigned two students to represent the country on a committee, they should be prepared to operate solo for two reasons. The first, as discussed in the What Would You Do? exercise, is the possibility that their committee partner may not participate in the conference. As such, they need to have their own wedge issue, fully researched, to promote on behalf of their home government. Hopefully, everyone in the delegation will avoid illness or personal emergency and the full complement of students will participate in all sessions. Even then, you want each student to have distinct wedge issues for the topics. When the committee breaks into caucus it is better to have two representatives for your country operating separately, putting together their own working group and simultaneously drafting distinct documents. This is the "two-for-one" effect of doubling up in committee. It can only happen, however, if students have their own wedge issue to promote.

The "pitch" happens early in the first topic caucus when your student approaches a small number of fellow delegates and invites them to work together. They'll begin with something along the lines of

Hi. I'm representing Poland and have an idea for a resolution that might interest you.

Would you like to meet to discuss it?

Once the delegate has the attention of the others, s/he must pitch the wedge issue that has been the focus of research for most of the semester. This is easier said than done and takes practice to get right. The student doesn't want to press too hard or come off as domineering but needs to convey that the idea being proposed has a high potential of becoming the basis for a resolution.

To hone their skills, put them on the hot seat. Divide the class into groups of three or four. Select one student from each group to be on the hot seat, ask the others to represent a different country for the exercise. Inform the students sitting in the hot seat that they will have 45 seconds to pitch their wedge issue and engender interest from the others to work on a resolution together. Remind them to introduce themselves by country name at the start of their pitch. When the time has expired, instruct the others in the group to ask questions about the wedge issue. Give them four minutes for group discussion and Q&A. Many of the questions asked will take the person on the hot seat by surprise, having not considered them before. This is an extremely important aspect of preparing for the wedge issue sales pitch. Select another student in each group to take the hot seat and repeat the exercise until all student-delegates have had the opportunity to pitch their wedge issue. At the conclusion of the exercise, debrief by asking what particularly difficult questions were asked. Continue to require students to raise their placards and be called upon before they speak. Answer the questions if possible or brainstorm with the class on the best way to respond should the same question be raised at the conference.

One of the most common questions asked of a student on the hot seat relates to funding their idea. Most wedge issues call for some form of action (online training system for teachers, solar kettles, refugee tracking app, etc.) which requires resources. Students should be made aware of the four funding sources for a project, as outlined below.

Funding Options		
1	Regular Budget	Funded through the UN Budget
2	Voluntary Contributions	Member-State Contributions
3	Corporate Sponsorship	Donations from Major Companies
4	Fundraising	Public Donations/Go Fund Me

The **Regular Budget (RB)** is the UN's general account that is made up of the annual dues paid by member-states. Membership in the United Nations requires each state to pay an annual fee, the amount is based on the country's "ability to pay." A General Assembly committee determines the membership fee for each country. According to the Charter, if a UN Member State falls two years in arrears, the country loses its vote in the General Assembly. Since its founding in 1945, the United States has received the highest dues assessment. As long as the committee being simulated receives its funding from the United Nations, the regular budget option is available. **Voluntary Contributions (VC)** are made by member states above and beyond the annual dues that they pay to retain membership in the United Nations. For every dollar that the United States pays in annual dues, it voluntarily contributes five dollars to various UN agencies and programmes. Unlike the regular budget, where diverting funds to cover a new venture comes at the expense of another, member-states can be asked to voluntarily contribute additional funds at any time for most any reason. Another funding option is to invite major companies to support the initiative through **Corporate Sponsorship (CS)**. Ted Turner, owner of Time Warner, Inc., donated $1 billion to the United

Nations in 2015. Large tech firms, especially, have market caps that are larger than several countries, making them prime targets for corporate sponsorship. Finally, a project being proposed at conference can be paid for by a general fundraising campaign, such as Go Fund Me.

Once students have been through the hot seat exercise, they will have a greater appreciation for the types of questions they may be peppered with during caucus negotiations. Let them know that they will return to the hot seat in week nine to present their wedge issue for their second committee topic.

Week 8B

Simulation: Revolution

A revolution is underway. The peasantry's demands are as follows:

1. The right to vote,
2. land reform,
3. secularism, and
4. taxes based on income rather than a flat tax.

Participants are divided into three groups as follows:

PEASANTRY: Composed of common citizens who demand change.
ARISTOCRACY: The wealthy class, owners of industry.
CLERGY: The religious group whose interest is protecting the church.

Pass a resolution that effectively ends the revolution. A resolution passes by simple majority of votes by individuals (not delegations). The failure to pass a resolution will lead to continued violence, destruction of property and the loss of human life.

Each participant may make one speech.

Time Limit: 60 minutes

Prep Material. One placard for each the three groups (Peasants, Aristocracy, Clergy).

Instructions. Assign students to the three groups using the formula below. Percentages do not need to be exact, simply make sure that the peasants have the largest number of students (votes) and the combined votes of the aristocracy and clergy is more than 50%.

>Peasants: 45%
>Aristocracy 35%
>Clergy   20%

Simulation Recap. The aristocracy and clergy are natural allies in this simulation. They are being targeted by the violence and generally agree that the demands being made by the peasants are contrary to their interests. They, after all, set up the social, political and economic order that is under attack. The combined vote of the aristocracy and clergy is more than the simple majority required to pass a resolution. The assignment, however, is not to pass a resolution but to "pass a resolution that effectively ends the revolution." For that to occur, the peasants must agree to the final document. In other words, solving a crisis on paper is significantly less impactful than reaching an accord that solves the problem on the ground.

There are three measures for how close to conference-ready your students are. The first is the division of work assignments within each group (peasants, aristocracy, clergy). By this point in the training protocol, the students should understand that they need to break up the required duties into three categories: document drafting, speech writing, negotiation. Successfully responding to a complicated and intense revolution mandates a division of labor, otherwise, the delegation will not be able to cover all aspects of the simulation. The second thing to look for is the extent to which the groups are willing to compromise to avoid further bloodshed. The clergy may resist secularism but concede voting rights and tax policy. The aristocracy will likely reject taxes based on income and land reform but may be willing to endorse secularism. While the peasantry has the largest number of voters in the simulation, the outcome usually is determined by which other group (clergy, aristocracy) makes the minimum number of concessions to engender support from the peasantry. Finally, carefully note if students encourage members of other groups to break away and vote differently than their group. While solidarity within groups is the norm, offers to individuals may entice them to break ranks and "vote their conscience." If the peasantry can peel away a few votes from both other groups, it may reach the simple-majority threshold while conceding less in the final document. At the conference, the logic follows, students should not think of the African bloc or European bloc, but instead explore separate deals with some members of those blocs to bring them from No to Abstain or Abstain to Yes on the document.

Week 9A

Final Research Binder Check
Return to the Hot Seat

The third binder check is taken at week nine and considers the portfolio wholistically. Begin by confirming that the binder is filled with information that addresses all areas of conference preparation. Verify that the binder is logically organized with labeled dividers and sub-dividers. You want the binders to be impressive in presentation, which is the final purpose of the binders. Beyond being a valuable resource to be used during deliberations, a well-organized and full binder sends a signal of preparation and seriousness to other student-delegates, the dais and the judges. Most students who participate in model diplomacy conferences are less than adequately prepared to accurately represent their assigned country on the topics under consideration. Many attend as members of student clubs with advisors but not instructors. Others attend conferences for social and tourism reasons. Finally, all our students have a multitude of responsibilities (assignments from other classes, work, family obligations, health issues, among others) that prevent them from being fully prepared for a competition. When those students see others with portfolios, they naturally gravitate towards them when the time comes for negotiations and resolution drafting. Research binders, in other words, give student-delegates an inherent advantage at conference.

With modern technology, it is wholly feasible for students today to store the information that they need in electronic form. The days of traveling hours in small groups to a United Nations depository of official documents, photocopying resolutions and using typewriters to draft speeches are a thing of the past. Today, students can locate most any document within a few seconds on their smartphones. Tablets can store thousands of pages of documents. I fully understand and appreciate that on a certain level, physical binders are a relic of a bygone era. Given, however, the value of monitoring student progress throughout the training protocol and the impact that a well-organized binder presents at the conference, I will continue to require portfolios.

The students return to the hot seat to practice making their pitch for their second topic's wedge issue. Turn up the heat in round two by instructing the students to be more aggressive and demanding during the question time. It is better to be thrown off balance in a class exercise than at the conference. If organized correctly, the hot seat will toughen the students and better prepare them for the rigors of committee battle.

Week 9B

Simulation: OPEC+ Summit

The Organization of Petroleum Exporting Countries (OPEC) sets oil production quotas for each of its members. Leaders of OPEC+ nations have gathered to set production quotas for next year. Current production quotas (in millions of barrels per day) are listed below.

Each nation has a number of votes that reflect this year's quote (1 vote per million barrels per day). OPEC has decided to increase production next year by 10 mbd. Barrel quotas must be in whole numbers, states may have their production quotas raised or lowered. Use the Quota Form to propose quota changes for each of the OPEC members. To be adopted, the proposed quota changes must receive a super majority (2/3) of all votes (48).

Time Limit: 60 minutes

OPEC+ Member	Current Production	Changes in Quota
Algeria	2	
Gabon	2	
Russia	9	
Iran	5	
Iraq	5	
Kuwait	3	
Nigeria	2	
Saudi Arabia	9	
Libya	3	
UAE	3	
Venezuela	3	
Equatorial Guinea	2	
Azerbaijan	2	
Congo	3	
Sudan	2	
South Sudan	2	
Mexico	3	
Bahrain	2	
Oman	2	
Brunei	2	
Kazakhstan	2	
Malaysia	2	
Total Production	72	+10

Prep Material. Placards for participating countries.

Instructions for the Chair. After 45 minutes of simulation, invite delegates to propose quota changes one at a time until a proposal is adopted. It is advisable to post the Oil Production Quota Form on the screen and note changes, if any, for each country. Before submitting the proposal to a vote, check the math to make sure that the additions total ten million barrels. If not, announce that the proposal is invalid and invite another delegate to make a proposal. Since the number of votes for each country varies (Saudi Arabia, 9; Malaysia, 2), it is best to use roll call to calculate an accurate tally. Forty-eight or more votes in favor are required for adoption.

Simulation Recap. Students enter this simulation with the skills and experience needed to work through almost any situation. The OPEC+ simulation is a diplomatic challenge wrapped in a mathematical puzzle. There are more than 100 combinations of votes that can reach the super-majority vote threshold to complete this task. The simulation is not only about oil production but voting power in the future as quotas determine votes. This adds even more risk to not achieving the preferred outcome for member-states.

Outcome	Best	Acceptable	Worst
Result	Gain a Barrel	No Quota Change	Lose a Barrel
Vote	Yes	Abstain	No

This simulation is distinct in that there are guaranteed winners and losers. With twenty-two participants and only ten additional barrels to be added to the current quota formula, a limited number of countries can gain in oil production. This means that many OPEC+ members will fall behind those that gained not only additional oil production rights but voting power the following year. Each delegate's goal at the onset of the simulation is to gain a barrel of oil production and the outcome that they hope to avoid is losing a barrel of production. This leads to what is referred to as band wagoning, whereby delegates move quickly to join what they believe is the emerging majority in hopes of not being left out of the quota increases. Once the like-minded group reaches its target quota increases, it has little need for the countries who will not gain in production quotas.

Week 10 A & B

Simulation: Korean Peninsula Crisis

Yesterday, North Korea declared that the 1953 Korean War Truce was nullified. It delivered an ultimatum to the United States and the Republic of Korea (ROK) demanding that they halt all joint military operations tonight by midnight (GMT). The statement, delivered via the Pyongyang News Agency, warned that a failure to heed the ultimatum would result in "…a catastrophic conflict of historic proportions."

The United Nations Security Council called an emergency meeting to address the rising tensions on the Korean Peninsula and to determine the proper steps to be taken. The United Nations Secretary General is reported to have made a personal plea to the United States and South Korea to announce a postponement of their joint military operations until the current crisis is resolved.

The Security Council is composed of fifteen member states, five of whom (China, France, Russia, United Kingdom, United States) have veto power. All UNSC resolutions require nine yes votes, including the concurring votes (yes or abstain) of the five permanent members. Japan, North Korea & South Korea are invited guests, they may not vote.

Fully debate and attempt to resolve the current crisis on the Korean Peninsula.

Time Limit: 120 minutes.

Prep Material. Placards for P5 Security Council members (China, France, Russia, United Kingdom, United States), Rotating 10 members (2 Western Europe, 1 Eastern Europe, 2 Africa, 3 Asia, 2 Latin America & the Caribbean) and three guests (Japan, Democratic People's Republic of Korea, Republic of South Korea).

Directions for the Chair. This simulation brings your students the closest to competition-level experience as they can get and completes the circle of required activities (formal speaking, caucus negotiation, resolution writing, document adoption) necessary for conference preparation. It is a long simulation, complex in its origins that evolves over the course of the Security Council session. At two hours in length, I use two class sessions to complete the crisis simulation with the first update (provided below) introduced at the 50-minute mark. The second update is provided at the beginning of the second 60-minute session. The time between the sessions should be used by the students to draft formal resolutions using the conference template. This is their first opportunity to practice drafting resolutions during a simulation, so it is important that the chair requires the students to download the resolution template and practice working on the shared document.

Korean Peninsula Crisis: Update I

Released at the 50-minute mark

It has been reported that a South Korean military frigate has been fired upon and destroyed in the vicinity of the Baengnyeong Island. The island was targeted by North Korea in an artillery attack before on November 23, 2010, resulting in four South Korean deaths and 19 injured. A rescue operation is currently underway.

Pyongyang denies any connection to the incident, however, both South Korea and the United States have accused North Korea of aggression and declared the disputed Yellow Sea area as a war zone. They have given North Korea 24 hours to remove all its naval vessels from the area and have reserved the right to use military force, if necessary, to secure the area.

Korean Peninsula Crisis: Update II

Released at the 60-minute mark

Profoundly complicating an already tense situation in East Asia, Chinese and Japanese warships exchanged gunfire early this morning around the disputed Senkaku Islands. A 1952 bilateral security treaty between Japan and the United States draws the USA even more deeply into the unfolding drama and tense environment of the region. The United Nations Security Council continues to convene in its emergency session to address the myriad problems in the area.

Simulation Recap. Explain to the students that what they experienced in this simulation, updates and changed circumstances, will not happen at the conference. Model diplomacy competitions, except for crisis simulations, "freeze" time a day or two before opening ceremonies. Therefore, changes in government or real-world developments are not considered and do not impact preparation leading up to the conference. The length of this simulation, particularly if the two sections are separated by days, allows students to thoroughly reflect on the resolutions that they are drafting. In the previous exercises, students had little time to draft conference-level resolutions due to time constraints. The value of this simulation, beyond resolution writing practice, is to force students into a discomfort zone while under the pressure of an impending deadline. They will face significant pressures at the conference, the more experience they have with facing them the better.

Week 11A

Exam

Below is a typical exam for a model diplomacy class that is a week or two away from the conference. It is a mix of country and topic information.

1. Country's formal name:
2. Geographic size (sq. miles):
3. Population size:
4. Per capita income: $
5. Capital:
6. Head of State (title/name):
7. Date of independence:
8. List of bordering states:
9. Year that the state joined the organization being simulated:
10. Official language(s):
11. Religion(s):
12. Flag (draw a picture and label colors):
13. Currency:
14. Your assigned committee:
15. List your assigned topics and the title of your wedge issue for each:

Topic 1:

Topic 2:

Which topic do you prefer? Explain why.

For each of your committee topics provide three sentences to promote your wedge issue.

Topic 1 Wedge Issue:

Topic 2 Wedge Issue:

Answer each of the following questions that might be posed to you by another delegate:
Why is your country taking a leading role on this issue?

Why should other countries care about what you are suggesting?

What is the Golden Rule of the program?

List the four funding options for your wedge issue.

1.
2.
3.
4.

List the member-states that are your closest allies and/or ones that you intend to seek out to form a working group.

Which countries, if any, does your assigned country not work with?

Week 11B & 12A

Simulation: Divided Island

Situation. Two United Nations peacekeepers were killed Monday on the island of Cyprus when the Jeep they were traveling in hit an improvised exploding device (IED). To date, 185 peacekeeper fatalities have occurred on the island, with less than 10% designated as malicious acts. It is unclear if the peacekeepers were the intended target of the bomb. The event indicates a possible escalation of violence by one of the sides in the long-simmering militarized dispute.

Background. Cyprus gained independence in 1960 from the United Kingdom, which maintains two military bases on the island. In 1964, the United Nations Security Council authorized a peacekeeping force (UNFICYP) to stabilize the capital city. In 1974, Turkey invaded Cyprus and gained control of approximately 1/3 of the island. The Turkish Republic of Northern Cyprus was established, however, only Turkey has extended recognition to the entity. UNFICYP was strengthened, enlarged and reassigned to the Green Line that divides Turkish from Cypriot forces, a demarcation that stretches from coast to coast. Since its inception, UNFICYP has operated on a six-month mandate that has been renewed twice annually since 1964. With a civilian-military contingent of 1,000 peacekeepers from two dozen countries, UNFICYP's expenses are paid for by the United Kingdom. London announced after the incident that it would no longer fully fund the operation and was considering a withdrawal of its peacekeepers.

Setting. The Security Council has called an emergency meeting to address the fluid situation in Cyprus. In addition to the fifteen members of the Council, representatives of the Republic of Cyprus and Northern Cypriot government have been invited to attend (without voting privileges).

Assignment. In separate resolutions, using the conference resolution template, address each of the following issues:

1. A response to the incident that claimed the lives of the peacekeepers,
2. A decision on the renewal of the six-month mandate, and
3. A new funding model.

Time Limit: 100 minutes, divided between two sessions.

Prep Material.   Placards for countries as follows: P5 members (China, France, Russia, UK, USA), R10 members (Africa: 3, Asia: 2, Latin American & the Caribbean: 2, WEOG: 2, Eastern Europe: 1), and one each for the two Cypriot delegates.

Instruction for the Chair: Each working group should organize itself into three sub-groups:

Drafting: Using the conference drafting template, this group frames out the basic principles of the working paper using a balance of preambular and operative clauses.

Speech Writing: Drafting of speeches reflecting the interests of the working group. Speeches should be able to convey the main aims of the group's document and expectations for the topics being addressed by the other working groups.

Inter-Group Caucus:These delegates are responsible for communicating with the members of the other working groups to remain knowledgeable of what they are drafting and to inform them of the substance of the document their group is working on.

This simulation stretches across two class periods, beginning at the end of week eleven and concluding at the beginning of week twelve. The interim, whether it is a long weekend or a single day, provides students the opportunity to carefully draft resolutions for each of the three assigned areas.

The Divided Island Crisis		
Week 11B	Interim	Week 12B
Form Three Caucus Groups Research Topics Formal Speeches Strategy Setting	In the days between sessions students should be working in their caucus groups to draft formal resolutions	Speeches Vote Hunting Amendments Final Voting

Recap: This is the second opportunity for students to practice resolution writing with adequate time for attention to detail and completeness. Ideally, the chair will set a deadline for submission of first drafts during the interim and review all documents for formatting compliance and acceptable content. At the conference, a dozen or more resolutions may be in progress in each committee. Student-delegates must not only concentrate on the document that their working group is drafting, but also be cognizant of the work being done by other groups. This simulation guarantees that three resolutions will be simultaneously drafted for final consideration. It is an excellent practice simulation for what they will experience at the conference.

Week 12B. Simulation

Tsunami

A 7.9 earthquake in the North Pacific Ocean has caused a major tsunami that has hit the disputed Kuril Islands. Populated by nearly 20,000 people, an immediate infusion of relief aid is needed to prevent a humanitarian disaster. Composed of 56 islands and reefs, the Kurils have been a point of contention between Russia, which administers them, and Japan, which historically has claimed the islands.

The Russian Federation immediately called for international assistance to save the Kuril population from ruin. Its only port in the vicinity, at Vladivostok, is ill-equipped to receive, process and direct aid to the victims. Japan and South Korea, on the other hand, have regional sea and airports capable of efficiently delivering aid to the islands. Russia, fearing that the involvement of its Pacific rim neighbors in a relief effort could threaten its hold on the islands, has demanded that its territory be exclusively used to conduct all aid relief operations.

Find a way to overcome Russian concerns over outside involvement and determine a means to deliver the needed resources to the islands within 24 hours to save the distressed population.

Using the resolution template provided in class, draft a document that is sufficiently supported to address the Kuril Island crisis. Resolutions require a 60% majority vote to be adopted.

Time Limit: 60 minutes.

Prep Material. Placards for each student are required, make sure to have students represent the states principally involved along with major and minor powers.

Recap. One last crisis that the students should be able to handle without difficulty. Having completed the twelve-week training protocol, your students are ready for the conference. Make certain to tell them that.

At the Conference

After months of preparation, the conference finally arrives. Delegations of students travel to the host city to put their training to the test. No longer will they be negotiating with peers that they have grown to know and trust well, at the conference they engage with a multitude of unknowns. It is highly suggested to hold an on-site meeting before the conference officially begins. This is an opportunity to touch base with everyone in your group to set expectations and remind the students of the challenge ahead. Following the guidelines and training protocol found in this guide should afford every student the opportunity to successfully represent their country and contribute to the drafting of an impressive resolution. There are, however, conference situations that are not fully and adequately addressed in the classroom. I divide these "situations" into three categories, providing both a description of the unexpected challenge and a means of resolving the problem.

The Expected

Participating in an academic conference presents several unavoidable challenges and disruptions that can be discussed in class but cannot be replicated at your home school. Travel plans can be disrupted, hotel rooms may not be ready, personalities clash under pressure and sleeping routines are altered when students share a single room. Succeeding at representing your country relies on more than academic knowledge of assigned countries and topics. Additionally, students must arrive at the conference well rested and mentally prepared for long committee sessions and the rigors of a multi-day simulation.

Conference participants gather for the first time as country representatives at the opening ceremony. The atmosphere is charged with excited student-delegates meeting one another and being formally welcomed to the conference by event organizers. Some students hand out business cards with their name, assigned country and committee, with many getting an early jump on negotiating before their first committee session begins. For faculty, it is wonderful to see the next generation of problem solvers intermingle and to think of the global challenges that the students will someday resolve. For many students, opening ceremonies are intimidating. Having prepared for the conference in a calm and nurturing classroom environment, maneuvering through the practice simulations with supportive classmates and being encouraged to make mistakes to improve their skills, at the opening ceremony they find themselves surrounded by hundreds, if not thousands, of students from all over the world. Understandably, they begin to wonder if they really are as prepared as their teacher has assured them for the past twelve weeks. It is fully expected that some of your students will feel overwhelmed by the opening ceremony environment. Before sending delegates into the room, I remind students of five things:

1. You are well prepared.
2. You've earned the right to be here.
3. Your assignment is not to be the dominant delegate in the room. Rather, it is to find a small working group and focus your attention and energy on your wedge issue.
4. Go in and have fun.
5. Repeat the Golden Rule: A Body in Motion, Tends to Stay in Motion. The best way to overcome conference jitters is to jump in and get the ball rolling.

When the opening ceremony concludes, the students make their way to their assigned committee room. Their first session goals remain the same as discussed in class: put your name on the speakers' list and identify your working group. From there, the conference falls into its normal routine of toggling between formal and informal sessions. Students who jump right in from the start of the session will find themselves well on their way to negotiating a respectable resolution by the end of the first committee session.

The second on-site group meeting should be held at the end of the first session, either by meeting with the students as a group or individually as they leave their committee rooms. It is less useful to ask open-ended questions, such as "How did it go?" than to home in on key points such as

"Were you able to get on the speakers' list?" and "Did you put together a working group for resolution drafting?" Remind the students that they have taken the first step in what will be a long process. They need to shift their focus from getting started to building on what they have established for the resolution writing and debate stages that will follow. Advise the students to remain nourished and hydrated so that they can maintain their work pace. At NMUN conferences (D.C., NYC, international), the first session of committees ends in the evening with the second session beginning the next day. In such instances, encourage the students to get as much rest as possible and maintain a healthy diet in preparation for the next day.

Fatigue, irritation with others, and nervousness are all challenges expected at the conference. Monitoring students is key to identifying minor issues and preventing them from turning into serious problems. Whether you have a small or large delegation, establishing clean lines of communication is essential. Modern communication, including cell phones and text messaging, has revolutionized the ability to monitor and check in on students at the conference. Students, however, are at times reluctant to communicate unfavorable news to their faculty advisor. For that reason, most programs assign head delegate status to one or more of their most reliable and mature students. The head delegate, whether assigned to a committee or not, serves as a link between students and the conference organizers. They attend meetings to receive information that needs to be passed on to students and can bring issues before the conference leadership team. Additionally, the head delegate is someone students can turn to if they are experiencing problems in committee as they are often more comfortable speaking with a fellow student than a faculty member. Head delegates then take on the responsibility of determining which issues the student can address, which requires intervention by the head delegate and which should come to the attention of the faculty. Finally, fellow delegates are important sources of information about their peers. Everyone should feel a responsibility to let the head delegate or faculty leader know if their committee partner or roommate isn't eating, hydrating or getting enough rest to maintain their health.

The Unexpected

There are aspects of model diplomacy that simply cannot be replicated in the classroom prior to the conference. For twelve weeks, the students have been working collaboratively in preparing for committee sessions. They have relied upon each other to complete tasks and have grown accustomed to a calm, and largely predictable, pattern of class sessions. When they join large numbers of students with varied backgrounds, personalities and interests, things can so sideways very quickly. Common challenges that students do not anticipate confronting at the conference are listed below.

The Hub Isn't Working

The days of raising a placard to gain the attention of the chair are quickly giving way to the conference "hub," a web-based platform that allows student-delegates to confirm their attendance, place their country name on the speakers' list, message other delegates, submit documents, propose amendments, request a right of reply, cast votes and find resources needed to efficiently participate in the diplomatic process. Most conference hotels offer free Wi-Fi in common areas, which allows students to connect to the hub. When large numbers of students join the hotel Wi-Fi, it is often overloaded if not overwhelmed. I advise my students to use their cell phone data rather than rely upon the hotel Wi-Fi with its limited bandwidth.

Additionally, hubs can experience technical difficulties such that they are not reliable. This forces the dais to revert to the old school means of recognizing delegates by requiring them to raise their placards to the called upon. In class, this is not a problem given the modest number of students. When the numbers exceed one hundred, it is a challenge for any chair to fairly and equitably call upon students and even more difficult to attain accurate votes on amendments and resolutions.

Not Being Recognized by the Chair

Well-prepared students enter the first committee session with speeches at the ready for agenda setting, topic one and topic two. Their speeches, drafted during the middle portion of the training protocol, have been delivered in class, revised and delivered again. Their first goal in session one is to get on the speakers' list and deliver their speech as planned. This can only happen, of course, if they are placed on the speakers' list. When the hub is working properly, this is not an issue as students can click a button to join the list. During times of technical difficulty or a weak Wi-Fi signal, frustration builds when students feel that they are not being recognized by the chair. If the problem persists, students should be encouraged to visit the dais during an informal session and request to be placed on the speakers' list and even ask if there is something different that they can do to be recognized. They must keep in mind that the members of the dais are constantly addressed by students with specific demands and that being extremely polite and understanding when speaking to committee organizers is very important.

The "Stolen" Idea

By following the training protocol outlined in this manual, students will enter the conference with a firm idea of what they intend to draft a resolution about. Their wedge issue has been extensively researched, practiced in the hot seat exercise, and their topic speeches are on point. Problems arise when more than one working group is drafting a resolution on the same or similar idea. Far too often, students assume that the other group "lifted" the idea from their position paper, speech or adopted the issue after hearing about it during informal session. Whether or not this is the case is secondary to the need to remediate the duplication. Students have three basic responses to this scenario. First, and preferably, they can approach the other working group and suggest collaboration. Rather than writing two resolutions that cover the same wedge issue, they can collectively draft one document. Students should keep in mind that once a working paper is submitted to the dais, it becomes the property of the committee as a whole and all members of the committee will vote on it. For this reason, expanding the working group from four delegates to eight or ten should be viewed as a positive step towards successfully adopting the document on the final vote. Additionally, the dais looks favorably upon students who solve problems amongst themselves rather than asking a conference official to step in. Second, your student can opt to draft a resolution on another issue, either a back-up idea brought to the conference, or an issue suggested by another member of the working group. It is important to discuss this option with all members of the working group as starting a new draft document is a dramatic and challenging direction to take. Finally, and least suggested, is to approach the dais and inform its members that your group's idea for a resolution was adopted by another group. This approach rarely works and generally leads to negative outcomes. The chair will likely encourage the students to sort things out with the other group, which is more difficult when that group's members learn that they have been accused of unethical behavior.

Merging

The goal of each committee is to consider and adopt a series of resolutions that address multiple aspects of the assigned topic. No matter how specific the topic, there will always be many angles that can be taken to address it. Assume for a moment that there is incontrovertible evidence that country X intentionally targeted and harmed a protected person (Red Cross worker) in clear violation of international law. Resolutions could be drafted on the specific event, accountability, repercussions for the violation, the underlying situation that gave rise to ICRC presence in the country, the protection of humanitarian workers, in general, and the role of the white helmets in conflict and disaster areas, among others. The breaking down of topics into subsections was discussed earlier in the chapter on wedge issues. With multiple resolutions being drafted by various working groups, overlapping of subject matter is frequent. When two (or more) working papers are submitted to the dais for consideration, groups with overlaps are often encouraged to merge their resolutions into a single document.

Merging resolutions is a difficult process. The number of delegates simultaneously drafting the compromise document can be high, students are under pressure to meet an impending deadline and tempers can flare. Students who spent the past several sessions carefully drafting their resolutions are often frustrated with the rapid merging of the documents into one that, in their opinion, is less elegant and specific than the document they drafted. Once the merging process has begun, there is little that can be done except to join the process and be ready to sacrifice content to reach a consensus on the new document.

The Conference Bully

Nothing is more frustrating to the well-prepared and disciplined student-delegate than a bully who substitutes assertiveness for collaboration. A unilateral claim to the right to take charge and direct informal caucus sessions happens for several reasons. The person taking the lead may assume that they are best suited for the job, or they may not be particularly prepared for debate, so they attempt to shut it down by directing others around. It may be a matter of personality or the result of pressure to win an award by showing leadership. A common tactic is for the bully to loudly announce that her or his regional grouping will be meeting in one corner of the room when the next caucus session begins. Once the group is assembled, the bully seeks to control the direction of the discourse and assigns tasks (research, speech writing, inter-bloc dialogue, document drafting, etc.) to sub-groups. I tell my students in class that if you are bothered by a domineering personality, others are bothered as well. The student can avoid falling under the influence of the bully by seeking out a small number of fellow delegates to work with.

The "Freeloader"

There will always be students who see the value of attaching their wagon to someone else's star. Rather than putting in the weeks of preparation and training in the lead up to the conference, they join groups to receive credit for the final product without materially contributing to the process. The most common freeloader approach is to visit multiple working groups and ask to be added as a sponsor to the document being drafted. If granted, the freeloader will have editing privileges and will claim credit for the work product. The best response to such a request is to state "We've been working on this document for several sessions and are not accepting new sponsors but would welcome you as a signatory." In other words, offer the student half a loaf and leave it to them to accept your generous offer.

The Grandstander

For those who do not want to exert the energy required of the bully or freeloader, there is always the option of grandstanding. This student delegate hangs on the periphery of the discussion while keeping an eye out for a member of the dais or a judge. When they see such a person approach, the grandstander will suddenly rise and begin to actively engage in the discussion for as long as the judge is in the vicinity. After which, they go back to scrolling their social media accounts. There is nothing wrong with gently calling out the grandstander by saying "You don't have to wait for a conference official to walk by to join in the conversation."

Pre-Drafted Resolutions

A central component of model diplomacy is the drafting of working papers and resolutions that resolve international problems and create opportunities for global society. At academic conferences, the resolutions emerge organically from the collaborative work of members of the committee. Unlike at the United Nations, where a topic can be addressed annually for decades with each year's document building modestly on the previous year's resolution, at model diplomacy conferences the students start anew each year. When a United Nations session ends, the next session begins immediately. As such, the diplomats in New York are cumulatively building on progress. At model diplomacy conferences, sessions are separated by fifty-one weeks and there is little cumulation from one year to the next. Nothing undermines the integrity of the drafting process more than students arriving at conference with a pre-drafted resolution. In the old days, students went to a designated room at the hotel where rows of typewriters were provided for drafting purposes. Conferences provided blank documents with a letterhead that ensured that the resolutions that came before the committee for consideration were drafted on site. Today, everyone attends the conference with a personal laptop computer where pre-drafted resolutions can be stored. The most obvious case of presenting a pre-drafted resolution occurred at the Model UN of the Far West when a student took out a document from their binder in the first committee session. Even without the holes punched on the pages, it was obviously not drafted at the conference. Rather than accusing the student of violating conference rules, the best reply is "We're starting a working paper as a group and will begin with a blank template."

The Use of Artificial Intelligence

The rise in popularity and availability of artificial intelligence (AI) presents both opportunities and perils in model diplomacy. Because it is increasingly integrated into computer software systems, at times it is difficult to even know if you are using artificial intelligence. While the use of AI can greatly assist a student in preparing for conferences by locating and synthesizing complex diplomatic and legal texts, it can also be detrimental to the intellectual development of students and undermine the integrity of the experience. For good reasons, AI is universally banned in respected academic conferences. It offers a short cut to the hard work required for preparation, allows students to draft speeches on complex topics in mere seconds and short-circuits the diplomatic dialogue needed to reach agreement. If a student suspects another of using AI in the drafting of a resolution, the best response is to state: "The dais runs all submitted documents through an AI screening software and invalidates all resolutions that test positive." It's a gentle way of calling someone out without making an accusation that is easy to deny and difficult to prove.

These Unknowns are incredibly frustrating for the well-prepared delegate. They must be psychologically prepared to address them to the best of their ability while remaining in diplomatic character. Calling out a bully, freeloader or grandstander too assertively and accusing a fellow delegate of bringing a pre-drafted resolution or using Artificial Intelligence can lead to grave consequences. The natural response of anyone violating the principles of the conference is to deny the allegations and counterattack. It is frustrating enough to deal with a domineering personality or an unethical person, adding a personal feud to the mix can ruin the experience.

The Serious

The safety of our students is the top priority of every team leader as well as the conference organizers. The number and quality of speeches delivered, resolutions passed, and awards received pales in comparison to the physical and mental well-being of members of the delegation. Over the course of four decades of leading students on domestic and international conference trips, I have visited more emergency rooms than I care to recall. While many of the crises could have been avoided if proper care had been taken by the students, there are times when no amount of safety protocol can keep every student safe. A few years ago in Washington, D.C., some of my students were walking through Georgetown when a person on a motor scooter lost control and ran over one of them. Emma suffered severe lacerations to the face, arms and legs. To make a very bad situation worse, the students decided not to call an ambulance. Instead, they took a taxi back to the hotel and used basic first aid to clean and wrap the wounds. They also declined to inform me of the situation, using the excuse that it was very late at night and didn't want to disturb me. When I saw the student the next morning, truly looking like she had been run over, I called for medical support to insure that she was more properly tended to. Another year, while waiting for our rooms to be ready in the conference hotel in New York, a student complained of severe pain in her foot. I took one look and realized that medical attention was needed, escorting her to a local ER. The soreness was caused by a splinter from the previous week and had turned into a staph infection. She needed a heavy regime of antibiotics, was required to keep her foot elevated when possible and was taken to a physician for follow-ups four times during the one-week conference. Her meals had to be brought to her and a temperature check every two hours was advised by the doctor. Had this student opted to muscle through the pain and not sought immediate medical treatment, she could have lost her leg. These are but a few of the myriad examples of students from my school facing life-threatening emergencies. I am confident that other veteran faculty advisors can relay similar health crises.

While some accidents and situations are unavoidable, there are precautions that can be taken by the team leader to minimize the likelihood of a medical emergency and/or mitigate the severity of the situation. Prior to departure, it is imperative that every advisor provide in writing the expectations for behavior and the limits of what students may do while at the conference. My list includes the following:

1. Call 9-1-1 immediately in the event of any medical emergency to yourself or others. If a student passes out from dehydration or exhaustion, assume the worst and call for help. Do not take chances with your or other people's health.

2. Contact the faculty leader as soon as you are off the phone with an emergency dispatch. When I chaperone one hundred students to a conference, it is impossible to maintain constant contact with all of them. Their willingness to communicate with me and their head delegates is essential and a hard requirement. I remind my students that my cell phone is on 24/7 at the conference and there is never a bad time to contact me about a serious matter.

3. Keep a close eye on each other and report any concerns before they escalate to something more dangerous.

4. The is a zero-tolerance policy for illegal drug use or underage drinking. I emphasize to my students that if they see someone from our school breaking this rule and fail to report it to the faculty advisor, the punishment will be the same for them as the one violating the rule. This creates a self-interest in reporting problematic behavior.

5. Every student must sleep in their assigned hotel room every night of the conference. I do not institute a curfew, as it is impossible to enforce, and do not conduct bed checks. Consistent with rule number four, if roommates do not report a missing student, they will be held accountable.

6. Clearly designate the areas of the host city where students are allowed to travel. In New York, I draw a line north at 100th street and circle the remainder of the island. If a student wants to go to a Yankee game in the Bronx, or visit a relative in Brooklyn, the faculty advisor must pre-approve the travel. Additionally, I require dates and times of the expected travel outside the allowed zone and expect a text message as soon as the student(s) return to Manhattan. Washington, D.C. is much more difficult to draw clear geographic lines. The conference hotel is in Virginia, so I cannot require students to restrict their travel to the District. Instead, I warn them of the pockets of the city where crime is most likely and strongly advise them to avoid those areas.

7. Students are not allowed to go out alone at night. If a student gets out of committee late and their peers have already left for a late dinner, he or she can always contact the head delegate or faculty advisor to walk together to a nearby establishment.

8. Keep nothing from the advisor. We can only be there for students if they communicate their concerns with us. In the 1990s, I had a student who fell off the map for two days. No one knew where she was and, without cell phones, there was little that I could do to locate her. I notified the police, called every hospital in the five boroughs and contacted her parents back in Florida. I placed the entire delegation on lock-down, meaning that no one was allowed to leave the hotel complex until she returned. It turns out that she was perfectly fine but had decided that the conference was not for her and decided to stay with relatives in Queens for a few days. She was shocked to learn how upset I was with her and the degree of animus she received from her fellow delegates who were required to pay a high price for her dereliction.

Rules are more likely respected when students clearly understand the consequences of breaking them. For that reason, I provide students with not only the list of rules but the grade deduction for each violation. As you will note from the grade sheet provided at the beginning of this manuscript, 10% (100 points out of 1000) of their final grade is conference participation. If a student misses an assigned session (opening ceremonies, committee session, closing ceremonies) without prior approval, they will suffer a 50-point (1/2 letter grade) deduction. Major violations, such as not returning to the hotel at night or violating the prohibition on drugs and alcohol, result in a 100-point (full letter grade) deduction and, in extreme cases, confinement to their hotel room for the remainder of the conference. If students act in an unprofessional fashion, a warning is issued followed by a twenty-five-point deduction for each infraction. For the record, the highest number of behavioral infractions for one student at a conference is twenty-seven.

When reviewing the rules and penalties for violations, it is important that you stress that they are in place to protect their safety and well-being. The rules are not designed to exert control over students, but rather to help them to understand boundaries and to minimize the likelihood of self-endangerment.

Closing Ceremony

After the final gavel falls, marking the adjournment of the committee until the next year, student-delegates gather one last time for a ceremony to review the accomplishments achieved, bid farewell to the interesting people that they met, and mark the conclusion of their efforts to resolve challenges that confound professional diplomats. Most, but not all, model diplomacy conferences announce awards, individual and delegation, at the closing ceremony. Typically, there are three categories of awards— Position Paper, Best Delegate in Committee and Delegation. The position paper awards are determined by a review of the documents that were submitted by the deadline and graded on format and content. Best Delegate awards are determined on the last day of the conference by popular vote in each committee. The chair will instruct delegates to cast votes for the two or three most deserving countries in committee, with those receiving the highest number of votes selected for the honor. Delegation awards are for countries represented at the conference. Established conferences will post the criteria for awards, including areas of evaluation, as well as the formula used to compare countries with differing numbers of committee assignments.

Activities Evaluated by Judges for Delegation Awards	
Positive	Negative
Arriving at the conference prepared	Unprepared for the conference
Attending all committee sessions	Tardy or absent from sessions
Openly and positively engaging others	Resistant to cooperation
In diplomatic & country character	Out of diplomatic & country character
Proper diplomatic discourse/language	Improper diplomatic discourse/language
Delivering prepared speeches	Declining to make speeches
Authoring resolutions	Not participating in resolution writing
Encouraging fellow delegates	Denigrating fellow delegates
Respecting protocol	Disrespecting protocol
Student-drafted documents	Artificial Intelligence drafted documents

Model diplomacy conferences may award one type of delegation award or offer awards at different levels. Typical of the latter are Outstanding Delegation, Distinguished Delegation and Honorable Mention. As a rule, awards at major conferences break down as indicated below.

Delegation Award		
Type	Description	Percentage
Outstanding	Truly exceptional representation of assigned country	10%
Distinguished	Exceptional representation of assigned country	20%
Honorable Mention	Impressive representation of assigned country	30%

If the percentage of delegations receiving awards is reflected in the above breakdown, half of all countries represented at the conference will not win an award. A delegation award at any level should be celebrated and the lack of awards should not be a sign of failure. It took my program ten years to receive its first delegation award—Honorable Mention for the Delegation from Turkmenistan. Since 2006, the Leon Charney Diplomacy Program at FAU has received more than eighty national and international awards. Programs take time to build and nurture, patience is always required.

As clear as the criteria for determining individual and delegation awards may be stated, the judging of student-delegates is somewhat opaque. After forty years of experience in model diplomacy conferences, as a student, graduate advisor and program director, I still cannot view a committee session and identify the judges. Logic has it that members of the dais (Chairs, Directors, Assistants and Staff) participate in judging, but others may be present and taking notes. The safest advice to give students is to assume that conference judges are everywhere and witness all behavior. The instruction of always being in character, in and out of committee session, is sound advice. At the end of the day, however, it isn't the number of awards received by your students that matters. It is the life lessons they have learned from the experience and the enduring friendships that they have made that are the true measure of success.

The Debrief

Having returned to your home university, it is important to hold a group session to discuss the conference with your students. The debrief serves many purposes. It allows students to share their experiences with you and their classmates. Even though everyone attended the same academic event, individual experiences will vary greatly from one committee to another and one student to the next. The debrief gives students an opportunity to share their views of what went well and what was disappointing with the team leader and their fellow delegates. Faculty, whose primary focus on site is the safety and well-being of their students, often miss the nuances of the conference. An anonymous survey can be distributed to gather data on student participation that can be shared with future delegations during the training protocol.

Survey of Conference Participation	
How many delegates were in your committee?	
How many speeches did you deliver?	
How many motions did you make?	
How many resolutions did you draft?	
How many of your resolutions were adopted?	
Did the committee start work on the 2nd topic?	
Did the committee finish the 2nd topic?	

The most important benefit of the debrief is program enhancement and improved future training. If you intend to participate in model diplomacy going forward, post-conference reviews provide insight into how to revise your training protocol. Aside from the core skills required of all conferences, model diplomacy preparation is not a one-size-fits-all formula. Some lessons fall flat and simulations don't always achieve their intended purpose. Adjustments in every system are essential to program growth and student success.

I begin the debriefing session by congratulating students on their successful completion of the conference. As instructors, we sometimes forget the pressure that students face to live up to lofty expectations, whether they are articulated by the instructor, their fellow students or expected of themselves. It is important to remind them how far they have travelled since that first class. In programs such as mine, where only new students to model diplomacy are registered, it is not difficult to take them back to the moment when they received their two-inch research binder and held their name placard for the first time. At the beginning of the semester, few felt confident being asked to draft a formal speech and deliver it in an impressive fashion. Diplomatic training provides lessons and hones skills useful for all vocations and walks of life, conference participation is something that they will remember long after they have graduated. Not long ago, the daughter of one of my first model diplomacy students introduced herself on the first day of class and told me that her mother still talks about her experience traveling with the delegation to New York and representing the university at Nationals. Listen to the stories that they recount and think about how their experiences can influence preparation for the next conference.

The next debriefing step is to discuss other schools and how they performed in committee. I start the conversation by posting the awards (delegation, position paper, best-delegate-in-committee) on the board and walk the class through them. I point to specific delegations who received the highest award and ask "What about Cameroon struck you as impressive? What did the U.K. do well and how can we replicate that success?" Some delegations stand out by delivering unconventional speeches, others make their mark by being effective facilitators of group negotiations, still others by demonstrating impressive writing skills. It is important for the team leader to catalog the responses of their students when articulating the success of other student delegates. Identify, as a group, your own delegation's strengths and weaknesses by surveying the students, either formally with a written exercise or through a free exchange of views.

Next, I put the twelve-week training protocol on the board. Moving from one week to the next, I ask students how important each exercise was to their preparation for the conference. Use the table presented below to make notations of what the students believe needs to change in future preparations. Ask for a show of placards for each item to quantify student responses.

Post-Conference Debrief & Future Training Revisions			
Skill	More	Less	Adjustments Needed
Speech Writing			
Public Speaking			
Simulations			
Map Quizzes			
Country Quizzes			
What Would You Do?			
Rules of Procedure			
Hot Seat Exercise			
Position Paper Drafting			
Resolution Writing			
Resolution Merging			
Research Binder			

Two areas of preparation that are commonly identified as in need of greater attention are resolution writing and position paper drafting. To address the drafting of resolutions in response to student suggestions, in recent years I spread two of the simulations across multiple class sessions. This affords them the opportunity to work on their resolutions, using the conference template, over a period longer than a single class session. Drafting position papers is the Achilles' heel of my program for two reasons. First, I do not have veteran model diplomacy students to rely on to lead the drafting of position papers or serve as mentors to new students. Writing award-winning position papers, like drafting impressive resolutions, requires experience that can only be gained from conference participation. Colleagues have informed me that their successful position paper strategy uses a multi-step process whereby veteran students review and provide feedback on papers drafted by students who are new to the experience. Second, the timeline for the final submission of position papers is extraordinarily tight for classes that begin only eight weeks before the due date. I introduce the concept of position papers in week three, not long after the students receive their committee assignments, and require drafts to be submitted in week seven. While one month seems to be plenty of time for students to draft two-page papers, in reality they are working on so many fundamental aspects of preparation (country knowledge, committee information, topic backgrounds, map quizzes, speech drafting, etc.), that most begin to work on their position papers a week before the deadline. This is understandable since it is impossible to draft a paper before the student has gained sufficient knowledge of the assigned country and its position on the topics.

It is important to remember that preparation time is finite. Expanding attention paid in one area or adding a new training assignment to another comes at the expense of some other area of preparation. I inform students that while we could spend more time focusing on position papers or resolution writing, other skill-building exercises would need to be shortened, if not eliminated. It is a delicate balance that we must maintain to provide students with the necessary understanding of all areas of preparation that need to be covered in a short period of time.

The final project assigned to my students, which takes place during exam sessions, is a small-group multimedia project titled *My Diplomacy Program Experience*. Students self-select into groups of three to create a four-minute video presentation that is shown to the class. Their target audience, to keep things on the serious side, is someone (parents, college dean, donor) not familiar with model diplomacy. In their video presentations, they are to relate how the program impacted them as students, young professionals and competitors. While all projects will review the conference itself, ranging from committee sessions to tourist visits to nights on the town, they also reference the training protocol, the required site visits and friends that they made. A graded exercise, the groups present their video projects to the class as a great way to wrap up the semester.

Funding your Program

Model diplomacy programs require resources. An instructor, or academic advisor, and physical space are needed no matter the size and sophistication of the program. For programs that participate in model diplomacy conferences, registration fees, travel and hotel rooms must be paid for. The cost of a program, of course, depends on its size and the conference that it opts to attend. With the proliferation of model diplomacy events across the nation, you can almost always find one to attend that is more economically efficient than taking the students long distances to a major conference. Operating within one's means is an essential element of a successful long-term program. It is difficult enough to request financial support from your school, if you underestimate costs and are forced to go back to ask for more funding to fill the gap it can ruin your prospects for assistance the following year.

The Leon Charney Diplomacy Program at Florida Atlantic University has an annual operating budget of $150,000. The market value of its eight endowed accounts exceeds $1 million, which produces an annual allocation of approximately one-third of our budget. The remaining funds are raised through donations from the community. This level of available resources allows us to take large delegations of students to Nationals in Washington in the fall and New York City in the spring. Travel teams, as explained in chapter one, attend a dozen or more conferences per academic year. Such a commitment requires a substantial amount of funding that can be counted on from one year to the next. Regardless of the type of program that you envision and the conference(s) that you plan on attending, financial resources will be needed.

Cost Calculator

The first step to meeting the financial needs of a program is to set a goal based upon a budget. Knowing the costs of conference participation provides a fundraising goal to meet. The key costs include conference registration, delegate fees, travel to and from the conference city and hotel rooms. Due to the large number of model diplomacy conferences held annually, the anticipated costs of attendance can be greatly reduced by opting to participate in a shorter conference, thus reducing the number of nights in the hotel. Attending a local or regional conference where ground transportation can be used instead of purchasing airfare for your students will also lower the financial burden on your program.

The tables below compare the cost of attending a model diplomacy conference at three levels (local, regional, national) for a delegation of eight students with one faculty advisor. The following cost estimates were used to calculate the total cost of attendance:

School Registration (x1)

Local	$25
Regional	$75
National	$150

Delegate/Advisor Fee (x9)

Local	$75
Regional	$100
National	$195

Hotel Rooms (3 rooms x # of nights)

Local	$0
Regional	$200
National	$300

Airfare (x9)

Local	$0
Regional	$250
National	$250

Three hotel rooms are required for the travel conferences, with the students assigned to quad rooms and the faculty advisor to a single room. The figures are based on the delegation arriving on the day of the opening ceremony and departing the evening of the closing ceremony. Air travel is assumed to be the same for the travel conferences.

Cost for Eight Students & One Faculty Advisor to Attend a Conference						
Type	# of Days	Registration	Delegate Fee	Hotel	Air	Total
Local	2	$25	$675	$0	$0	$700
Regional	3	$75	$900	$1,200	$2,250	$4,425
National	7	$150	$1,755	$5,400	$2,250	$9,555

The costs range from under $100 per student for a local conference, where airfare and hotel are not needed, to $553 for a short regional conference to $1,194 for a national conference. International conferences, such as those offered annually by NMUN, are usually more expensive due to longer flights and passport/visa costs. Model UN groups with limited funding should consider attending a local conference to relieve the financial pressures associated with fundraising for expensive conferences. It is better to begin modestly and move up the ladder than get caught short of funding for a major expenditure.

Funding Models

There are two basic models for funding a program, self-funded and sponsored. A self-funded program, as its name implies, does not rely on school or university funding to operate. Since its inception in 1996, the program that I direct has been fully self-funded. It is not that my university declined to offer financial support, rather it was out of my desire to maintain full control over operations that can only happen when you are not underwritten by your school or university. At times, I wondered if the decision to raise program funds through community support was the right choice. There have been very difficult financial stretches when it was not altogether clear if the program could consistently travel to Nationals. When funds were low, I selected fewer students to attend, arranged to arrive on the day the conference opened and departed the same day that the conference ended to reduce hotel expenses. We made our way to the conference hotel from JFK airport on long, uncomfortable commuter trains, all the while dressed in formal attire since we were arriving only hours before the opening ceremony. At other times, the program has been so flush with funds that we could travel with extremely large delegations, arrive a day early and attend conferences abroad. While most model diplomacy programs fundraise, including those that receive funding from their schools, at FAU our program is solely funded by donations from the community.

For those seeking funding from their institution, be it a high school or university, documentation will need to be prepared. Administrators, before committing resources, want to be certain of what they are investing in. A clear statement of purpose, including the value of the program to not only students but the institution, is essential. A timeline and list of resources needed must be included in a written budget as well as the anticipated outcome of the endeavor. Since you want to receive as much as possible from your institution and there are always financial overages, lean towards the high side when you are drafting your budget. University-based programs, in addition to requesting support from their unit chairs or college deans, may be eligible to receive funding from student government. University students pay social activity fees with each credit hour taken, those funds are controlled by student government which may use them for many purposes. There is a rule in the state of Florida that limits student government funding to social and cultural activities, with student governments precluded by law from funding academic activities. Since my program is clearly academic, operating through five college classes per year, it is not eligible for student government funding. This limitation on the availability of funds from student government is avoided if you are operating a club that is registered with student government. Your meetings and prep sessions will need to take place outside of the formal classroom to avoid running afoul of the restrictive funding rules. I have several colleagues who actively recruit student government members into their programs in order to enhance the chance of being awarded sufficient funds to operate their programs.

There are two problems associated with institutional funding and are the main reasons that I opted not to ask my department, college or university for financial support. The first, discussed above, is control over operational decisions. If a bureaucrat funds you, they have a vested interest in your program and expect to play a role in making important decisions. The second problem is reliability over a long period of time. While the program that I established in 1996 was modest, to say the least, I had visions of a much larger and sophisticated program, one that could operate year-round and be nationally competitive. What I did not want to risk was suspending the program every time that the university ran into financial difficulties and was forced to cut its budget. As important as model diplomacy programs are to its students and instructors, they fall far down the priority list of deans and provosts, meaning that funding for them is not a primary concern. Had my program relied principally on university funding to operate, it would have suspended operations following the Great Recession (2008) and COVID epidemic (2020-21). No one wants a start-and-stop program because suspension is no way to build a large, established program. For this reason, even if you do receive funding from your institution, you will probably want to raise funds yourself.

Principles of Fundraising

It is important to think strategically before planning tactics. Trial and error are a big part of most long-term endeavors, fundraising included. While there is no one-size-fits-all approach to raising money, there are some principles that I have learned over the course of time of asking for support from members of the South Florida community.

Branding. The first fundraising tip is to think from the perspective of the donor and how they perceive your program. Helping in that matter are the labels that you use to describe your program. Branding is no longer the singular domain of corporations who want to put their product in the most favorable light, it is found everywhere. Schools and universities brand their image, even countries are hiring branding experts to improve public relations. Your model diplomacy program should be no different. When I founded the program at my university, I named it Model United Nations like most every similar program in the nation. As an academic, I felt that the title accurately described what it was and what it did. When the Great Recession hit in 2008, it represented an existential threat to the Model UN program. It wasn't a financial crisis due to the inevitable university budget cuts that followed, after all my program did not receive university financial support. Rather it was the result of a new policy enacted by the provost that was caused by the difficult economic environment. Seeking to stretch university resources as far as possible, she set a minimum registration of twenty-four students for upper-division courses. The university simply could not make ends meet with low-enrollment classes. Because the program was small, the new rule required me to double the number of students in the MUN course. This meant that I needed to double the amount of donations received. To do this, my first step was rebranding. I stopped thinking about its label from the perspective of what the students were doing and more about how it was perceived by potential donors. I conducted a quasi-scientific survey of word association. Three groups of people (students, professors, community members) were asked what they associated with the term "model united nations." The most common responses were "fun" and "travel." While model United Nations is fun and does involve travel, such perceptions are not overly conducive to fundraising. The next set of words that I asked about was "diplomacy program." The responses were highly positive, including "serious" and "training." From that point onward, the title "Diplomacy Program" was used with our motto: "Training Tomorrow's Leaders Today" prominently displayed on all fliers and webpages. The purpose of using this verbiage was to convey seriousness and instill in the minds of donors that they were investing in the next generation of diplomats and problem solvers. Both the number of donations and the value of the average donation increased significantly, allowing the program to meet the higher registration threshold and survive the financial crisis. Branding is key to successful fundraising.

Return on Investment of Energy & Time. Most fundraising efforts are modest, selling brownies or putting out collection boxes for passersby to drop a dollar in. Charity car washes and yard sales are also common fundraising ventures for model diplomacy groups. A more sophisticated and energy-intensive strategy is to host a conference for area schools, charging fees that are used to fund your group's conference trip. The problem is that the payout for these fundraisers is fairly low in comparison to the amount of time and energy required. This is especially true of hosting a conference, which takes far more effort than one might assume. For thirteen years (1999-2012), we hosted the annual South Florida Model United Nations conference. The event was open to high school, college and university students. At its peak, more than 200 area students participated in the weekend MUN conference. It was not until year five that we broke even and at its apex the conference never cleared more than a few hundred dollars in profit. Given the expense of hosting the conference (room rentals, print material, parking, security etc.), it was clear that the SFMUN was not going to provide the financial resources needed to fund our travel team.

Any fundraising effort must show a substantial return (profit) on the investment (energy/time). By far, the most efficient fundraising effort with the highest payout-to-investment ratio is also the simplest: asking people to donate money to your program. It is better to ask ten people to donate $1,000 with a 20% success rate than to host brownie sales and car washes every weekend for month. If you are not comfortable directly asking people for a donation, do it indirectly by setting up a Go Fund Me page for your group.

Fundraise from a Position of Strength. Fundraising is common for all sorts of activities, ranging from athletics to the arts to academics. A common incentive employed to gain a donation is guilt. This is done by telling prospective donors that your group needs funds to be able to travel to a tournament, game or conference, or to host a music camp for less privileged children. Without the funds, the pitch continues, the activity may have to be canceled. People with the capacity to make donations are immediately put on the defensive by such a tactic. Donating to rescue a program from failing leads to the assumption that the future will hold much of the same. No one wants to be guilted into making a sizeable donation, much less feeling like they will be on the hook the following year, to rescue the program again. Instead, encourage people to buy into your successful program. Tell them (1) how impacting what you do is on students and (2) that all funds are directly used for program operations.

Provide Options to Donors. Asking for unspecified levels of support for your students to attend an academic conference is a poor fundraising strategy. Consider offering donors a tiered status list. Donations at a certain level result in the donor's name listed as a Bronze Supporter. At a higher level, they are a Silver Supporter, with Gold Supporter for the highest level. For some programs with modest needs, the levels may be set at $50, $75 and $100. Programs with greater needs may set the three bars at $100, $500 and $1,000. There is no cost to the program as lists can be printed inexpensively, but such incentives work. The key when setting the "ask" levels is to read your donor target market and be ready to adjust upward or downward to find the sweet spot. But never be shy to think big.

Endowed Scholarship. Universities and colleges maintain endowments that benefit students, teachers, sports and social programs administered by the school. Each university establishes a baseline, or minimum, donation required to create an endowed account. Funds deposited in the endowed account are referred to as the core, from which earnings are generated through investment of the funds. Donors may continue to contribute to the core over time, which increases the amount of earnings in up markets. Annually, the endowed fund pays out to the recipient program a portion of the account's earnings.

The beneficiary of an endowed account is determined by the donor in consultation with the university. Large, endowed gifts may provide support for infrastructure, such as a building, programs or target individual students. The gift agreement, signed by all parties, specifically outlines the permissible uses of the funds. An endowed donation is sometimes a naming gift since the donor's name is attached to the building, program or scholarship.

There are several things to keep in mind relating to endowed gifts. First, faculty are severely limited in the role that they play in landing large donations. Endowed gifts are the domain of the college's development office, the professionals who have access to information and training in fundraising that faculty do not. Second, endowed account annual payouts are limited by university, state or federal guidelines. Public colleges and universities normally limit allocations to 3%-5% of the core, or original gift. Therefore, a $25,000 endowed gift will pay out between $750 (3%) and $1,250 (5%) yearly. Third, endowed gifts must hibernate for one calendar year to build up earnings to pay out during the second year. As a result, the benefit of an endowed gift is delayed. Finally, endowed account allocations are contingent on market growth. The funds are invested in stocks, bonds, CDs, and a multitude of other investments options. When earnings are positive, the endowment pays out. In a down market, there may be no allocation until the market recovers.

The "Empty" Scholarship. While the FAU endowed accounts that support the Diplomacy Program provide the basis for program activities and expenses, it makes up only about one-third of annual expenses to take large numbers of students to major conferences each year. The remainder of the budget is filled out with what I refer to as empty scholarships. For a set amount, donors can create an annual scholarship that bears their name. The funds are deposited into the program's cash, or expendable, account for immediate use. A student is selected to receive the scholarship and adds the line to their resume. The funds, however, are not directed towards the recipient student. Instead, they are used for general expenses for the program. I find that donors prefer for the funds to be controlled by the program leader and used specifically for program needs as opposed to being awarded to a single student. When I first introduced the scholarship offer, the amount was set at $1,000. Over time, the minimum required rose to the current level of $5,000. The annual scholarship is flexible in that donors can support the program without an obligation to continue, should their life experience and needs change. It is also fruitful to package scholarships to donors, offering two scholarships for $8,000. There is no expense for the program and all funds received are immediately available for official use. It is advisable to create a separate scholarship webpage where donors can see their named scholarship and its recipient. Donors often see this as an opportunity to honor loved ones, create a memorial scholarship or, in one case, turn it into an annual birthday gift for their spouse.

Sponsorship. A third donor option is to sponsor a student. For the Washington, D.C. conference, I set the sponsorship level at $750 as that covers registration, fees, hotel and airfare for one student on average. For the more expensive New York conference, the sponsorship level is $1,000. Aside from the lower donor amount, this differs from the scholarship option in that no named award is announced. Sponsorship is an appealing opportunity for people with limited means to support student education through the program. I like to think of sponsorships as entry gifts, in that over time as the donor's appreciation of what the program offers grows, they can be invited to consider moving up their support to scholarship level.

Host a Donor Event. Over time, the number of people who financially support your program should grow. If not, you must rethink your fundraising model. Hosting an annual on-campus gathering, such as a luncheon or "Meet the Students" event, for current and prospective donors can expand the donor base. Invite a small number of your students to attend to make brief presentations about their experiences in the program and their career aspirations. Members of the public will be impressed with the public speaking skills that you have taught your students. Connecting donors with their scholarship recipients is a highly effective means of anchoring your support base to your program. Always provide a List of Donation Options card to each participant and ask your development officer to individually contact each attendee to encourage a donation. People do not always like to be asked for a donation, but they are more likely to support your program when you ask them for their assistance.

Every program has its own financial needs based upon a wide range of variables, from the size of the delegation to the costs of the attending a conference. Teachers and faculty who lead programs are given varying degrees of freedom and authority to raise funds for their students. It is important for program leaders to first communicate with their school's administration for guidelines before starting to raise funds through charitable donations.

Conclusion

The principles, exercises and simulations found in this training manual are the result of decades of trial and error in the diplomacy classes that I teach. Some, such as Fatal Decision (week 2) and Trust or Betrayal (week 6), date to my first class in 1996 and have not changed over the years. Others (Korean Crisis, week 10; Divided Island, weeks 11 & 12) were developed more recently at the suggestion of students to add more resolution writing practice to the protocol. Garnering the feedback from your students after the conference plays an important role in revising and improving your own training protocol for future classes. It is never as easy as simply adding a new exercise or simulation to the game plan because doing so comes at the expense of an activity that must be deleted or abbreviated. Many instructors using this manual will opt for more attention paid to position papers. Others will view the rules of parliamentary procedure as the best path to successful conference participation. The protocol described herein is not designed as a one-size-fits-all. Every class, club or program is distinct in what it prefers to emphasize and can easily modify the training schedule to suit their needs and interests. We encourage our students to make mistakes to improve, the same advice is suitable for program leaders.

The purpose of this manual is to provide model United Nations programs of all sizes, shapes and ambitions with a training protocol that will prepare students to successfully participate in academic conferences. Based upon more than four decades of model diplomacy experience, the material offered should be of use for new and established programs. It is my intent that this manual promotes the positive aspects of skills building that will serve students well in their model diplomacy experiences and prepare them for the challenges they will face in their professional lives.

United Nations Charter

Preamble

WE THE PEOPLES OF THE UNITED NATIONS DETERMINED

to save succeeding generations from the scourge of war, which twice in our lifetime has brought untold sorrow to mankind, and to reaffirm faith in fundamental human rights, in the dignity and worth of the human person, in the equal rights of men and women and of nations large and small, and to establish conditions under which justice and respect for the obligations arising from treaties and other sources of international law can be maintained, and to promote social progress and better standards of life in larger freedom,

AND FOR THESE ENDS

to practice tolerance and live together in peace with one another as good neighbours, and to unite our strength to maintain international peace and security, and to ensure, by the acceptance of principles and the institution of methods, that armed force shall not be used, save in the common interest, and to employ international machinery for the promotion of the economic and social advancement of all peoples,

HAVE RESOLVED TO COMBINE OUR EFFORTS TO ACCOMPLISH THESE AIMS.

Accordingly, our respective Governments, through representatives assembled in the city of San Francisco, who have exhibited their full powers found to be in good and due form, have agreed to the present Charter of the United Nations and do hereby establish an international organization to be known as the United Nations.

Chapter I: Purposes and Principles

Article 1

The Purposes of the United Nations are:

1. To maintain international peace and security, and to that end: to take effective collective measures for the prevention and removal of threats to the peace, and for the suppression of acts of aggression or other breaches of the peace, and to bring about by peaceful means, and in conformity with the principles of justice and international law, adjustment or settlement of international disputes or situations which might lead to a breach of the peace;
2. To develop friendly relations among nations based on respect for the principle of equal rights and self-determination of peoples, and to take other appropriate measures to strengthen universal peace;
3. To achieve international co-operation in solving international problems of an economic, social, cultural, or humanitarian character, and in promoting and encouraging respect for human rights and for fundamental freedoms for all without distinction as to race, sex, language, or religion; and
4. To be a centre for harmonizing the actions of nations in the attainment of these common ends.

Article 2

The Organization and its Members, in pursuit of the Purposes stated in Article 1, shall act in accordance with the following Principles.

1. The Organization is based on the principle of the sovereign equality of all its Members.
2. All Members, in order to ensure to all of them the rights and benefits resulting from membership, shall fulfill in good faith the obligations assumed by them in accordance with the present Charter.
3. All Members shall settle their international disputes by peaceful means in such a manner that international peace and security, and justice, are not endangered.
4. All Members shall refrain in their international relations from the threat or use of force against the territorial integrity or political independence of any state, or in any other manner inconsistent with the Purposes of the United Nations.

5. All Members shall give the United Nations every assistance in any action it takes in accordance with the present Charter, and shall refrain from giving assistance to any state against which the United Nations is taking preventive or enforcement action.

6. The Organization shall ensure that states which are not Members of the United Nations act in accordance with these Principles so far as may be necessary for the maintenance of international peace and security.

7. Nothing contained in the present Charter shall authorize the United Nations to intervene in matters which are essentially within the domestic jurisdiction of any state or shall require the Members to submit such matters to settlement under the present Charter; but this principle shall not prejudice the application of enforcement measures under Chapter VII.

Chapter II: Membership

Article 3

The original Members of the United Nations shall be the states which, having participated in the United Nations Conference on International Organization at San Francisco, or having previously signed the Declaration by United Nations of 1 January 1942, sign the present Charter and ratify it in accordance with Article 110.

Article 4

1. Membership in the United Nations is open to all other peace-loving states which accept the obligations contained in the present Charter and, in the judgment of the Organization, are able and willing to carry out these obligations.

2. The admission of any such state to membership in the United Nations will be effected by a decision of the General Assembly upon the recommendation of the Security Council.

Article 5

A Member of the United Nations against which preventive or enforcement action has been taken by the Security Council may be suspended from the exercise of the rights and privileges of membership by the General Assembly upon the recommendation of the Security Council. The exercise of these rights and privileges may be restored by the Security Council.

Article 6

A Member of the United Nations which has persistently violated the Principles contained in the present Charter may be expelled from the Organization by the General Assembly upon the recommendation of the Security Council.

Chapter III: Organs

Article 7

1. There are established as principal organs of the United Nations: a General Assembly, a Security Council, an Economic and Social Council, a Trusteeship Council, an International Court of Justice and a Secretariat.
2. Such subsidiary organs as may be found necessary may be established in accordance with the present Charter.

Article 8

The United Nations shall place no restrictions on the eligibility of men and women to participate in any capacity and under conditions of equality in its principal and subsidiary organs.

Chapter IV: The General Assembly

Article 9

1. The General Assembly shall consist of all the Members of the United Nations.
2. Each Member shall have not more than five representatives in the General Assembly.

Article 10

The General Assembly may discuss any questions or any matters within the scope of the present Charter or relating to the powers and functions of any organs provided for in the present Charter, and, except as provided in Article 12, may make recommendations to the Members of the United Nations or to the Security Council or to both on any such questions or matters.

Article 11

1. The General Assembly may consider the general principles of co-operation in the maintenance of international peace and security, including the principles governing disarmament and the regulation of armaments, and may make recommendations with regard to such principles to the Members or to the Security Council or to both.
2. The General Assembly may discuss any questions relating to the maintenance of international peace and security brought before it by any Member of the United Nations, or by the Security Council, or by a state which is not a Member of the United Nations in accordance with Article 35, paragraph 2, and, except as provided in Article 12, may make recommendations with regard to any such questions to the state or states concerned or to the Security Council or to both. Any such question on which action is necessary shall be referred to the Security Council by the General Assembly either before or after discussion.
3. The General Assembly may call the attention of the Security Council to situations which are likely to endanger international peace and security.
4. The powers of the General Assembly set forth in this Article shall not limit the general scope of Article 10.

Article 12

1. While the Security Council is exercising in respect of any dispute or situation the functions assigned to it in the present Charter, the General Assembly shall not make any recommendation with regard to that dispute or situation unless the Security Council so requests.
2. The Secretary-General, with the consent of the Security Council, shall notify the General Assembly at each session of any matters relative to the maintenance of international peace and security which are being dealt with by the Security Council and shall similarly notify the General Assembly, or the Members of the United Nations if the General Assembly is not in session, immediately the Security Council ceases to deal with such matters.

Article 13

1. The General Assembly shall initiate studies and make recommendations
   for the purpose of:
   1. promoting international co-operation in the political field and
      encouraging the progressive development of international law and
      its codification;
   2. promoting international co-operation in the economic, social,
      cultural, educational, and health fields, and assisting in the
      realization of human rights and fundamental freedoms for all
      without distinction as to race, sex, language, or religion.
2. The further responsibilities, functions and powers of the General
   Assembly with respect to matters mentioned in paragraph 1 (b) above
   are set forth in Chapters IX and X.

Article 14

Subject to the provisions of Article 12, the General Assembly may
recommend measures for the peaceful adjustment of any situation,
regardless of origin, which it deems likely to impair the general welfare or
friendly relations among nations, including situations resulting from a
violation of the provisions of the present Charter setting forth the Purposes
and Principles of the United Nations.

Article 15

1. The General Assembly shall receive and consider annual and special
   reports from the Security Council; these reports shall include an account
   of the measures that the Security Council has decided upon or taken to
   maintain international peace and security.
2. The General Assembly shall receive and consider reports from the other
   organs of the United Nations.

Article 16

The General Assembly shall perform such functions with respect to
the international trusteeship system as are assigned to it under Chapters
XII and XIII, including the approval of the trusteeship agreements for
areas not designated as strategic.

Article 17

1. The General Assembly shall consider and approve the budget of the Organization.
2. The expenses of the Organization shall be borne by the Members as apportioned by the General Assembly.
3. The General Assembly shall consider and approve any financial and budgetary arrangements with specialized agencies referred to in Article 57 and shall examine the administrative budgets of such specialized agencies with a view to making recommendations to the agencies concerned.

Article 18

1. Each member of the General Assembly shall have one vote.
2. Decisions of the General Assembly on important questions shall be made by a two-thirds majority of the members present and voting. These questions shall include: recommendations with respect to the maintenance of international peace and security, the election of the non-permanent members of the Security Council, the election of the members of the Economic and Social Council, the election of members of the Trusteeship Council in accordance with paragraph 1 (c) of Article 86, the admission of new Members to the United Nations, the suspension of the rights and privileges of membership, the expulsion of Members, questions relating to the operation of the trusteeship system, and budgetary questions.
3. Decisions on other questions, including the determination of additional categories of questions to be decided by a two-thirds majority, shall be made by a majority of the members present and voting.

Article 19

A Member of the United Nations which is in arrears in the payment of its financial contributions to the Organization shall have no vote in the General Assembly if the amount of its arrears equals or exceeds the amount of the contributions due from it for the preceding two full years. The General Assembly may, nevertheless, permit such a Member to vote if it is satisfied that the failure to pay is due to conditions beyond the control of the Member.

Article 20

The General Assembly shall meet in regular annual sessions and in such special sessions as occasion may require. Special sessions shall be convoked by the Secretary-General at the request of the Security Council or of a majority of the Members of the United Nations.

Article 21

The General Assembly shall adopt its own rules of procedure. It shall elect its President for each session.

Article 22

The General Assembly may establish such subsidiary organs as it deems necessary for the performance of its functions.

Chapter V: The Security Council

Article 23

1. The Security Council shall consist of fifteen Members of the United Nations. The Republic of China, France, the Union of Soviet Socialist Republics, the United Kingdom of Great Britain and Northern Ireland, and the United States of America shall be permanent members of the Security Council. The General Assembly shall elect ten other Members of the United Nations to be non-permanent members of the Security Council, due regard being specially paid, in the first instance to the contribution of Members of the United Nations to the maintenance of international peace and security and to the other purposes of the Organization, and also to equitable geographical distribution.
2. The non-permanent members of the Security Council shall be elected for a term of two years. In the first election of the non-permanent members after the increase of the membership of the Security Council from eleven to fifteen, two of the four additional members shall be chosen for a term of one year. A retiring member shall not be eligible for immediate re-election.
3. Each member of the Security Council shall have one representative.

Article 24

1. In order to ensure prompt and effective action by the United Nations, its
    Members confer on the Security Council primary responsibility for the
    maintenance of international peace and security, and agree that in
    carrying out its duties under this responsibility the Security Council acts
    on their behalf.
2. In discharging these duties the Security Council shall act in accordance
    with the Purposes and Principles of the United Nations. The specific
    powers granted to the Security Council for the discharge of these duties
    are laid down in Chapters VI, VII, VIII, and XII.
3. The Security Council shall submit annual and, when necessary, special
    reports to the General Assembly for its consideration.

Article 25

The Members of the United Nations agree to accept and carry out the
decisions of the Security Council in accordance with the present Charter.

Article 26

In order to promote the establishment and maintenance of
international peace and security with the least diversion for armaments of
the world's human and economic resources, the Security Council shall be
responsible for formulating, with the assistance of the Military Staff
Committee referred to in Article 47, plans to be submitted to the Members
of the United Nations for the establishment of a system for the regulation
of armaments.

Article 27

1. Each member of the Security Council shall have one vote.
2. Decisions of the Security Council on procedural matters shall be made
    by an affirmative vote of nine members.
3. Decisions of the Security Council on all other matters shall be made by
    an affirmative vote of nine members including the concurring votes of
    the permanent members; provided that, in decisions under Chapter VI,
    and under paragraph 3 of Article 52, a party to a dispute shall abstain
    from voting.

Article 28

1. The Security Council shall be so organized as to be able to function continuously. Each member of the Security Council shall for this purpose be represented at all times at the seat of the Organization.
2. The Security Council shall hold periodic meetings at which each of its members may, if it so desires, be represented by a member of the government or by some other specially designated representative.
3. The Security Council may hold meetings at such places other than the seat of the Organization as in its judgment will best facilitate its work.

Article 29

The Security Council may establish such subsidiary organs as it deems necessary for the performance of its functions.

Article 30

The Security Council shall adopt its own rules of procedure, including the method of selecting its President.

Article 31

Any Member of the United Nations which is not a member of the Security Council may participate, without vote, in the discussion of any question brought before the Security Council whenever the latter considers that the interests of that Member are specially affected.

Article 32

Any Member of the United Nations which is not a member of the Security Council or any state which is not a Member of the United Nations, if it is a party to a dispute under consideration by the Security Council, shall be invited to participate, without vote, in the discussion relating to the dispute. The Security Council shall lay down such conditions as it deems just for the participation of a state which is not a Member of the United Nations.

Chapter VI: Pacific Settlement of Disputes

Article 33

1. The parties to any dispute, the continuance of which is likely to endanger the maintenance of international peace and security, shall, first of all, seek a solution by negotiation, enquiry, mediation, conciliation, arbitration, judicial settlement, resort to regional agencies or arrangements, or other peaceful means of their own choice.
2. The Security Council shall, when it deems necessary, call upon the parties to settle their dispute by such means.

Article 34

The Security Council may investigate any dispute, or any situation which might lead to international friction or give rise to a dispute, in order to determine whether the continuance of the dispute or situation is likely to endanger the maintenance of international peace and security.

Article 35

1. Any Member of the United Nations may bring any dispute, or any situation of the nature referred to in Article 34, to the attention of the Security Council or of the General Assembly.
2. A state which is not a Member of the United Nations may bring to the attention of the Security Council or of the General Assembly any dispute to which it is a party if it accepts in advance, for the purposes of the dispute, the obligations of pacific settlement provided in the present Charter.
3. The proceedings of the General Assembly in respect of matters brought to its attention under this Article will be subject to the provisions of Articles 11 and 12.

Article 36

1. The Security Council may, at any stage of a dispute of the nature referred to in Article 33 or of a situation of like nature, recommend appropriate procedures or methods of adjustment.

2. The Security Council should take into consideration any procedures for the settlement of the dispute which have already been adopted by the parties.
3. In making recommendations under this Article the Security Council should also take into consideration that legal disputes should as a general rule be referred by the parties to the International Court of Justice in accordance with the provisions of the Statute of the Court.

Article 37

1. Should the parties to a dispute of the nature referred to in Article 33 fail to settle it by the means indicated in that Article, they shall refer it to the Security Council.
2. If the Security Council deems that the continuance of the dispute is in fact likely to endanger the maintenance of international peace and security, it shall decide whether to take action under Article 36 or to recommend such terms of settlement as it may consider appropriate.

Article 38

Without prejudice to the provisions of Articles 33 to 37, the Security Council may, if all the parties to any dispute so request, make recommendations to the parties with a view to a pacific settlement of the dispute.

Chapter VII: Action with Respect to Threats to the Peace, Breaches of the Peace, and Acts of Aggression

Article 39

The Security Council shall determine the existence of any threat to the peace, breach of the peace, or act of aggression and shall make recommendations, or decide what measures shall be taken in accordance with Articles 41 and 42, to maintain or restore international peace and security.

Article 40

In order to prevent an aggravation of the situation, the Security Council may, before making the recommendations or deciding upon the measures provided for in Article 39, call upon the parties concerned to comply with such provisional measures as it deems necessary or desirable. Such provisional measures shall be without prejudice to the rights, claims, or position of the parties concerned. The Security Council shall duly take account of failure to comply with such provisional measures.

Article 41

The Security Council may decide what measures not involving the use of armed force are to be employed to give effect to its decisions, and it may call upon the Members of the United Nations to apply such measures. These may include complete or partial interruption of economic relations and of rail, sea, air, postal, telegraphic, radio, and other means of communication, and the severance of diplomatic relations.

Article 42

Should the Security Council consider that measures provided for in Article 41 would be inadequate or have proved to be inadequate, it may take such action by air, sea, or land forces as may be necessary to maintain or restore international peace and security. Such action may include demonstrations, blockade, and other operations by air, sea, or land forces of Members of the United Nations.

Article 43

1. All Members of the United Nations, in order to contribute to the maintenance of international peace and security, undertake to make available to the Security Council, on its call and in accordance with a special agreement or agreements, armed forces, assistance, and facilities, including rights of passage, necessary for the purpose of maintaining international peace and security.

2. Such agreement or agreements shall govern the numbers and types of forces, their degree of readiness and general location, and the nature of the facilities and assistance to be provided.

3. The agreement or agreements shall be negotiated as soon as possible on the initiative of the Security Council. They shall be concluded between the Security Council and Members or between the Security Council and groups of Members and shall be subject to ratification by the signatory states in accordance with their respective constitutional processes.

Article 44

When the Security Council has decided to use force it shall, before calling upon a Member not represented on it to provide armed forces in fulfilment of the obligations assumed under Article 43, invite that Member, if the Member so desires, to participate in the decisions of the Security Council concerning the employment of contingents of that Member's armed forces.

Article 45

In order to enable the United Nations to take urgent military measures, Members shall hold immediately available national air-force contingents for combined international enforcement action. The strength and degree of readiness of these contingents and plans for their combined action shall be determined within the limits laid down in the special agreement or agreements referred to in Article 43, by the Security Council with the assistance of the Military Staff Committee.

Article 46

Plans for the application of armed force shall be made by the Security Council with the assistance of the Military Staff Committee.

Article 47

1. There shall be established a Military Staff Committee to advise and assist the Security Council on all questions relating to the Security Council's

military requirements for the maintenance of international peace and security, the employment and command of forces placed at its disposal, the regulation of armaments, and possible disarmament.

2. The Military Staff Committee shall consist of the Chiefs of Staff of the permanent members of the Security Council or their representatives. Any Member of the United Nations not permanently represented on the Committee shall be invited by the Committee to be associated with it when the efficient discharge of the Committee's responsibilities requires the participation of that Member in its work.

3. The Military Staff Committee shall be responsible under the Security Council for the strategic direction of any armed forces placed at the disposal of the Security Council. Questions relating to the command of such forces shall be worked out subsequently.

4. The Military Staff Committee, with the authorization of the Security Council and after consultation with appropriate regional agencies, may establish regional sub-committees.

Article 48

1. The action required to carry out the decisions of the Security Council for the maintenance of international peace and security shall be taken by all the Members of the United Nations or by some of them, as the Security Council may determine.

2. Such decisions shall be carried out by the Members of the United Nations directly and through their action in the appropriate international agencies of which they are members.

Article 49

The Members of the United Nations shall join in affording mutual assistance in carrying out the measures decided upon by the Security Council.

Article 50

If preventive or enforcement measures against any state are taken by the Security Council, any other state, whether a Member of the United Nations or not, which finds itself confronted with special economic problems arising from the carrying out of those measures shall have the right to consult the Security Council with regard to a solution of those problems.

Article 51

Nothing in the present Charter shall impair the inherent right of individual or collective self-defence if an armed attack occurs against a Member of the United Nations, until the Security Council has taken measures necessary to maintain international peace and security. Measures taken by Members in the exercise of this right of self-defence shall be immediately reported to the Security Council and shall not in any way affect the authority and responsibility of the Security Council under the present Charter to take at any time such action as it deems necessary in order to maintain or restore international peace and security.

Chapter VIII: Regional Arrangements

Article 52

1. Nothing in the present Charter precludes the existence of regional arrangements or agencies for dealing with such matters relating to the maintenance of international peace and security as are appropriate for regional action provided that such arrangements or agencies and their activities are consistent with the Purposes and Principles of the United Nations.
2. The Members of the United Nations entering into such arrangements or constituting such agencies shall make every effort to achieve pacific settlement of local disputes through such regional arrangements or by such regional agencies before referring them to the Security Council.
3. The Security Council shall encourage the development of pacific settlement of local disputes through such regional arrangements or by such regional agencies either on the initiative of the states concerned or by reference from the Security Council.
4. This Article in no way impairs the application of Articles 34 and 35.

Article 53

1. The Security Council shall, where appropriate, utilize such regional arrangements or agencies for enforcement action under its authority. But

no enforcement action shall be taken under regional arrangements or by regional agencies without the authorization of the Security Council, with the exception of measures against any enemy state, as defined in paragraph 2 of this Article, provided for pursuant to Article 107 or in regional arrangements directed against renewal of aggressive policy on the part of any such state, until such time as the Organization may, on request of the Governments concerned, be charged with the responsibility for preventing further aggression by such a state.

2.   The term enemy state as used in paragraph 1 of this Article applies to any state which during the Second World War has been an enemy of any signatory of the present Charter.

Article 54

The Security Council shall at all times be kept fully informed of activities undertaken or in contemplation under regional arrangements or by regional agencies for the maintenance of international peace and security.

Chapter IX:
International Economic and Social Cooperation

Article 55

With a view to the creation of conditions of stability and well-being which are necessary for peaceful and friendly relations among nations based on respect for the principle of equal rights and self-determination of peoples, the United Nations shall promote:

1.   higher standards of living, full employment, and conditions of economic and social progress and development;
2.   solutions of international economic, social, health, and related problems; and international cultural and educational cooperation; and
3.   universal respect for, and observance of, human rights and fundamental freedoms for all without distinction as to race, sex, language, or religion.

Article 56

All Members pledge themselves to take joint and separate action in co-operation with the Organization for the achievement of the purposes set forth in Article 55.

Article 57

1. The various specialized agencies, established by intergovernmental agreement and having wide international responsibilities, as defined in their basic instruments, in economic, social, cultural, educational, health, and related fields, shall be brought into relationship with the United Nations in accordance with the provisions of Article 63.
2. Such agencies thus brought into relationship with the United Nations are hereinafter referred to as specialized agencies.

Article 58

The Organization shall make recommendations for the co-ordination of the policies and activities of the specialized agencies.

Article 59

The Organization shall, where appropriate, initiate negotiations among the states concerned for the creation of any new specialized agencies required for the accomplishment of the purposes set forth in Article 55.

Article 60

Responsibility for the discharge of the functions of the Organization set forth in this Chapter shall be vested in the General Assembly and, under the authority of the General Assembly, in the Economic and Social Council, which shall have for this purpose the powers set forth in Chapter X.

Chapter X: The Economic and Social Council

Article 61

1. The Economic and Social Council shall consist of fifty-four Members of the United Nations elected by the General Assembly.
2. Subject to the provisions of paragraph 3, eighteen members of the Economic and Social Council shall be elected each year for a term of three years. A retiring member shall be eligible for immediate re-election.
3. At the first election after the increase in the membership of the Economic and Social Council from twenty-seven to fifty-four members, in addition to the members elected in place of the nine members whose term of office expires at the end of that year, twenty-seven additional members shall be elected. Of these twenty-seven additional members, the term of office of nine members so elected shall expire at the end of one year, and of nine other members at the end of two years, in accordance with arrangements made by the General Assembly.
4. Each member of the Economic and Social Council shall have one representative.

Article 62

1. The Economic and Social Council may make or initiate studies and reports with respect to international economic, social, cultural, educational, health, and related matters and may make recommendations with respect to any such matters to the General Assembly to the Members of the United Nations, and to the specialized agencies concerned.
2. It may make recommendations for the purpose of promoting respect for, and observance of, human rights and fundamental freedoms for all.
3. It may prepare draft conventions for submission to the General Assembly, with respect to matters falling within its competence.
4. It may call, in accordance with the rules prescribed by the United Nations, international conferences on matters falling within its competence.

Article 63

1. The Economic and Social Council may enter into agreements with any of the agencies referred to in Article 57, defining the terms on which the agency concerned shall be brought into relationship with the United

Nations. Such agreements shall be subject to approval by the General Assembly.

2. It may co-ordinate the activities of the specialized agencies through consultation with and recommendations to such agencies and through recommendations to the General Assembly and to the Members of the United Nations.

Article 64

1. The Economic and Social Council may take appropriate steps to obtain regular reports from the specialized agencies. It may make arrangements with the Members of the United Nations and with the specialized agencies to obtain reports on the steps taken to give effect to its own recommendations and to recommendations on matters falling within its competence made by the General Assembly.
2. It may communicate its observations on these reports to the General Assembly.

Article 65

The Economic and Social Council may furnish information to the Security Council and shall assist the Security Council upon its request.

Article 66

1. The Economic and Social Council shall perform such functions as fall within its competence in connection with the carrying out of the recommendations of the General Assembly.
2. It may, with the approval of the General Assembly, perform services at the request of Members of the United Nations and at the request of specialized agencies.
3. It shall perform such other functions as are specified elsewhere in the present Charter or as may be assigned to it by the General Assembly.

Article 67

1. Each member of the Economic and Social Council shall have one vote.
2. Decisions of the Economic and Social Council shall be made by a majority of the members present and voting.

Article 68

The Economic and Social Council shall set up commissions in economic and social fields and for the promotion of human rights, and such other commissions as may be required for the performance of its functions.

Article 69

The Economic and Social Council shall invite any Member of the United Nations to participate, without vote, in its deliberations on any matter of particular concern to that Member.

Article 70

The Economic and Social Council may make arrangements for representatives of the specialized agencies to participate, without vote, in its deliberations and in those of the commissions established by it, and for its representatives to participate in the deliberations of the specialized agencies.

Article 71

The Economic and Social Council may make suitable arrangements for consultation with non-governmental organizations which are concerned with matters within its competence. Such arrangements may be made with international organizations and, where appropriate, with national organizations after consultation with the Member of the United Nations concerned.

Article 72

1.   The Economic and Social Council shall adopt its own rules of procedure, including the method of selecting its President.

2. The Economic and Social Council shall meet as required in accordance
    with its rules, which shall include provision for the convening of
    meetings on the request of a majority of its members.

Chapter XI: Declaration Regarding Non-Self-Governing Territories

Article 73

Members of the United Nations which have or assume responsibilities
for the administration of territories whose peoples have not yet attained a
full measure of self-government recognize the principle that the interests
of the inhabitants of these territories are paramount, and accept as a sacred
trust the obligation to promote to the utmost, within the system of
international peace and security established by the present Charter, the
well-being of the inhabitants of these territories, and, to this end:

1. to ensure, with due respect for the culture of the peoples concerned, their
    political, economic, social, and educational advancement, their just
    treatment, and their protection against abuses;
2. to develop self-government, to take due account of the political
    aspirations of the peoples, and to assist them in the progressive
    development of their free political institutions, according to the
    particular circumstances of each territory and its peoples and their
    varying stages of advancement;
3. to further international peace and security;
4. to promote constructive measures of development, to encourage
    research, and to co-operate with one another and, when and where
    appropriate, with specialized international bodies with a view to the
    practical achievement of the social, economic, and scientific purposes
    set forth in this Article; and
5. to transmit regularly to the Secretary-General for information purposes,
    subject to such limitation as security and constitutional considerations
    may require, statistical and other information of a technical nature
    relating to economic, social, and educational conditions in the territories
    for which they are respectively responsible other than those territories to
    which Chapters XII and XIII apply.

Article 74

Members of the United Nations also agree that their policy in respect of the territories to which this Chapter applies, no less than in respect of their metropolitan areas, must be based on the general principle of good-neighbourliness, due account being taken of the interests and well-being of the rest of the world, in social, economic, and commercial matters.

Chapter XII: International Trusteeship System

Article 75

The United Nations shall establish under its authority an international trusteeship system for the administration and supervision of such territories as may be placed thereunder by subsequent individual agreements. These territories are hereinafter referred to as trust territories.

Article 76

The basic objectives of the trusteeship system, in accordance with the Purposes of the United Nations laid down in Article 1 of the present Charter, shall be:

1. to further international peace and security;
2. to promote the political, economic, social, and educational advancement of the inhabitants of the trust territories, and their progressive development towards self-government or independence as may be appropriate to the particular circumstances of each territory and its peoples and the freely expressed wishes of the peoples concerned, and as may be provided by the terms of each trusteeship agreement;
3. to encourage respect for human rights and for fundamental freedoms for all without distinction as to race, sex, language, or religion, and to encourage recognition of the interdependence of the peoples of the world; and
4. to ensure equal treatment in social, economic, and commercial matters for all Members of the United Nations and their nationals, and also equal treatment for the latter in the administration of justice, without prejudice to the attainment of the foregoing objectives and subject to the provisions of Article 80.

Article 77

1. The trusteeship system shall apply to such territories in the following categories as may be placed thereunder by means of trusteeship agreements:
    1. territories now held under mandate;
    2. territories which may be detached from enemy states as a result of the Second World War; and
    3. territories voluntarily placed under the system by states responsible for their administration.
2. It will be a matter for subsequent agreement as to which territories in the foregoing categories will be brought under the trusteeship system and upon what terms.

Article 78

The trusteeship system shall not apply to territories which have become Members of the United Nations, relationship among which shall be based on respect for the principle of sovereign equality.

Article 79

The terms of trusteeship for each territory to be placed under the trusteeship system, including any alteration or amendment, shall be agreed upon by the states directly concerned, including the mandatory power in the case of territories held under mandate by a Member of the United Nations, and shall be approved as provided for in Articles 83 and 85.

Article 80

1. Except as may be agreed upon in individual trusteeship agreements, made under Articles 77, 79, and 81, placing each territory under the trusteeship system, and until such agreements have been concluded, nothing in this Chapter shall be construed in or of itself to alter in any manner the rights whatsoever of any states or any peoples or the terms of existing international instruments to which Members of the United Nations may respectively be parties.
2. Paragraph 1 of this Article shall not be interpreted as giving grounds for delay or postponement of the negotiation and conclusion of agreements

for placing mandated and other territories under the trusteeship system as provided for in Article 77.

Article 81

The trusteeship agreement shall in each case include the terms under which the trust territory will be administered and designate the authority which will exercise the administration of the trust territory. Such authority, hereinafter called the administering authority, may be one or more states or the Organization itself.

Article 82

There may be designated, in any trusteeship agreement, a strategic area or areas which may include part or all of the trust territory to which the agreement applies, without prejudice to any special agreement or agreements made under Article 43.

Article 83

1. All functions of the United Nations relating to strategic areas, including the approval of the terms of the trusteeship agreements and of their alteration or amendment shall be exercised by the Security Council.
2. The basic objectives set forth in Article 76 shall be applicable to the people of each strategic area.
3. The Security Council shall, subject to the provisions of the trusteeship agreements and without prejudice to security considerations, avail itself of the assistance of the Trusteeship Council to perform those functions of the United Nations under the trusteeship system relating to political, economic, social, and educational matters in the strategic areas.

Article 84

It shall be the duty of the administering authority to ensure that the trust territory shall play its part in the maintenance of international peace and security. To this end the administering authority may make use of volunteer forces, facilities, and assistance from the trust territory in carrying out the obligations towards the Security Council undertaken in this regard by the administering authority, as well as for local defence and the maintenance of law and order within the trust territory.

Article 85

1. The functions of the United Nations with regard to trusteeship agreements for all areas not designated as strategic, including the approval of the terms of the trusteeship agreements and of their alteration or amendment, shall be exercised by the General Assembly.
2. The Trusteeship Council, operating under the authority of the General Assembly shall assist the General Assembly in carrying out these functions.

Chapter XIII: The Trusteeship Council

Article 86

1. The Trusteeship Council shall consist of the following Members of the United Nations:
    1. those Members administering trust territories;
    2. such of those Members mentioned by name in Article 23 as are not administering trust territories; and
    3. as many other Members elected for three-year terms by the General Assembly as may be necessary to ensure that the total number of members of the Trusteeship Council is equally divided between those Members of the United Nations which administer trust territories and those which do not.
2. Each member of the Trusteeship Council shall designate one specially qualified person to represent it therein.

Article 87

The General Assembly and, under its authority, the Trusteeship Council, in carrying out their functions, may:

1. consider reports submitted by the administering authority;
2. accept petitions and examine them in consultation with the administering authority;
3. provide for periodic visits to the respective trust territories at times agreed upon with the administering authority; and

4. take these and other actions in conformity with the terms of the trusteeship agreements.

Article 88

The Trusteeship Council shall formulate a questionnaire on the political, economic, social, and educational advancement of the inhabitants of each trust territory, and the administering authority for each trust territory within the competence of the General Assembly shall make an annual report to the General Assembly upon the basis of such questionnaire.

Article 89

1. Each member of the Trusteeship Council shall have one vote.
2. Decisions of the Trusteeship Council shall be made by a majority of the members present and voting.

Article 90

1. The Trusteeship Council shall adopt its own rules of procedure, including the method of selecting its President.
2. The Trusteeship Council shall meet as required in accordance with its rules, which shall include provision for the convening of meetings on the request of a majority of its members.

Article 91

The Trusteeship Council shall, when appropriate, avail itself of the assistance of the Economic and Social Council and of the specialized agencies in regard to matters with which they are respectively concerned.

Chapter XIV: The International Court of Justice

Article 92

The International Court of Justice shall be the principal judicial organ of the United Nations. It shall function in accordance with the annexed

Statute, which is based upon the Statute of the Permanent Court of International Justice and forms an integral part of the present Charter.

Article 93

1.   All Members of the United Nations are ipso facto parties to the Statute of the International Court of Justice.
2.   A state which is not a Member of the United Nations may become a party to the Statute of the International Court of Justice on conditions to be determined in each case by the General Assembly upon the recommendation of the Security Council.

Article 94

1.   Each Member of the United Nations undertakes to comply with the decision of the International Court of Justice in any case to which it is a party.
2.   If any party to a case fails to perform the obligations incumbent upon it under a judgment rendered by the Court, the other party may have recourse to the Security Council, which may, if it deems necessary, make recommendations or decide upon measures to be taken to give effect to the judgment.

Article 95

Nothing in the present Charter shall prevent Members of the United Nations from entrusting the solution of their differences to other tribunals by virtue of agreements already in existence or which may be concluded in the future.

Article 96

1.   The General Assembly or the Security Council may request the International Court of Justice to give an advisory opinion on any legal question.
2.   Other organs of the United Nations and specialized agencies, which may at any time be so authorized by the General Assembly, may also request advisory opinions of the Court on legal questions arising within the scope of their activities.

Chapter XV: The Secretariat

Article 97

The Secretariat shall comprise a Secretary-General and such staff as the Organization may require. The Secretary-General shall be appointed by the General Assembly upon the recommendation of the Security Council. He shall be the chief administrative officer of the Organization.

Article 98

The Secretary-General shall act in that capacity in all meetings of the General Assembly, of the Security Council, of the Economic and Social Council, and of the Trusteeship Council, and shall perform such other functions as are entrusted to him by these organs. The Secretary-General shall make an annual report to the General Assembly on the work of the Organization.

Article 99

The Secretary-General may bring to the attention of the Security Council any matter which in his opinion may threaten the maintenance of international peace and security.

Article 100

1. In the performance of their duties the Secretary-General and the staff shall not seek or receive instructions from any government or from any other authority external to the Organization. They shall refrain from any action which might reflect on their position as international officials responsible only to the Organization.
2. Each Member of the United Nations undertakes to respect the exclusively international character of the responsibilities of the Secretary-General and the staff and not to seek to influence them in the discharge of their responsibilities.

Article 101

1. The staff shall be appointed by the Secretary-General under regulations established by the General Assembly.
2. Appropriate staffs shall be permanently assigned to the Economic and Social Council, the Trusteeship Council, and, as required, to other organs of the United Nations. These staffs shall form a part of the Secretariat.
3. The paramount consideration in the employment of the staff and in the determination of the conditions of service shall be the necessity of securing the highest standards of efficiency, competence, and integrity. Due regard shall be paid to the importance of recruiting the staff on as wide a geographical basis as possible.

Chapter XVI: Miscellaneous Provisions

Article 102

1. Every treaty and every international agreement entered into by any Member of the United Nations after the present Charter comes into force shall as soon as possible be registered with the Secretariat and published by it.
2. No party to any such treaty or international agreement which has not been registered in accordance with the provisions of paragraph 1 of this Article may invoke that treaty or agreement before any organ of the United Nations.

Article 103

In the event of a conflict between the obligations of the Members of the United Nations under the present Charter and their obligations under any other international agreement, their obligations under the present Charter shall prevail.

Article 104

The Organization shall enjoy in the territory of each of its Members such legal capacity as may be necessary for the exercise of its functions and the fulfilment of its purposes.

Article 105

1. The Organization shall enjoy in the territory of each of its Members such privileges and immunities as are necessary for the fulfilment of its purposes.
2. Representatives of the Members of the United Nations and officials of the Organization shall similarly enjoy such privileges and immunities as are necessary for the independent exercise of their functions in connection with the Organization.
3. The General Assembly may make recommendations with a view to determining the details of the application of paragraphs 1 and 2 of this Article or may propose conventions to the Members of the United Nations for this purpose.

Chapter XVII: Transitional Security Arrangements

Article 106

Pending the coming into force of such special agreements referred to in Article 43 as in the opinion of the Security Council enable it to begin the exercise of its responsibilities under Article 42, the parties to the Four-Nation Declaration, signed at Moscow, 30 October 1943, and France, shall, in accordance with the provisions of paragraph 5 of that Declaration, consult with one another and as occasion requires with other Members of the United Nations with a view to such joint action on behalf of the Organization as may be necessary for the purpose of maintaining international peace and security.

Article 107

Nothing in the present Charter shall invalidate or preclude action, in relation to any state which during the Second World War has been an enemy of any signatory to the present Charter, taken or authorized as a result of that war by the Governments having responsibility for such action.

Chapter XVIII: Amendments

Article 108

Amendments to the present Charter shall come into force for all Members of the United Nations when they have been adopted by a vote of two thirds of the members of the General Assembly and ratified in accordance with their respective constitutional processes by two thirds of the Members of the United Nations, including all the permanent members of the Security Council.

Article 109

1. A General Conference of the Members of the United Nations for the purpose of reviewing the present Charter may be held at a date and place to be fixed by a two-thirds vote of the members of the General Assembly and by a vote of any nine members of the Security Council. Each Member of the United Nations shall have one vote in the conference.
2. Any alteration of the present Charter recommended by a two-thirds vote of the conference shall take effect when ratified in accordance with their respective constitutional processes by two thirds of the Members of the United Nations including all the permanent members of the Security Council.
3. If such a conference has not been held before the tenth annual session of the General Assembly following the coming into force of the present Charter, the proposal to call such a conference shall be placed on the agenda of that session of the General Assembly, and the conference shall be held if so decided by a majority vote of the members of the General Assembly and by a vote of any seven members of the Security Council.

Chapter XIX: Ratification and Signature

Article 110

1. The present Charter shall be ratified by the signatory states in accordance with their respective constitutional processes.
2. The ratifications shall be deposited with the Government of the United States of America, which shall notify all the signatory states of each

deposit as well as the Secretary-General of the Organization when he has been appointed.

3. The present Charter shall come into force upon the deposit of ratifications by the Republic of China, France, the Union of Soviet Socialist Republics, the United Kingdom of Great Britain and Northern Ireland, and the United States of America, and by a majority of the other signatory states. A protocol of the ratifications deposited shall thereupon be drawn up by the Government of the United States of America which shall communicate copies thereof to all the signatory states.

4. The states signatory to the present Charter which ratify it after it has come into force will become original Members of the United Nations on the date of the deposit of their respective ratifications.

Article 111

The present Charter, of which the Chinese, French, Russian, English, and Spanish texts are equally authentic, shall remain deposited in the archives of the Government of the United States of America. Duly certified copies thereof shall be transmitted by that Government to the Governments of the other signatory states.

In Faith Whereof the representatives of the Governments of the United Nations have signed the present Charter. DONE at the city of San Francisco the twenty-sixth day of June, one thousand nine hundred and forty-five.

Index

www.ingramcontent.com/pod-product-compliance
Lightning Source LLC
Chambersburg PA
CBHW050239270326
41914CB00041BA/2046/J